Isolation
and
Security

The Contributors

WILLIAM R. ALLEN

University of California
at Los Angeles

RICHARD N. CURRENT

Woman's College of the
University of North Carolina

ALEXANDER DeCONDE

Duke University

ROBERT H. FERRELL

Indiana University

WILLIAM L. NEUMANN

Goucher College

KENNETH W. THOMPSON

The Rockefeller Foundation

J. CHALMERS VINSON

University of Georgia

Ideas and interests in twentieth-century
American foreign policy

Isolation

and

Security

Edited by ALEXANDER DECONDE

DUKE UNIVERSITY PRESS · *Durham, North Carolina* · 1957

Cambridge University Press, London, N.W.1, England
Library of Congress Catalogue Card No. 57-13022

Printed in the United States of America
By the Seeman Printery, Inc., Durham, N. C.

Preface

THE ESSAYS in this book were completed during an Interuniversity Summer Research Seminar held at Duke University from June 4 to July 28, 1956. Sponsored by the Social Science Research Council, the seminar brought together a group of scholars from different institutions who had a previous active and common interest in American diplomatic history, particularly in certain related ideas in twentieth-century foreign policy. While the seminar emphasized individual research and exchange of ideas, the authors felt that the essays, though exploratory, might be published together and prove of interest to a wider audience than that reached by the usual professional journal.

Speaking for all the seminar members, I thank the Social Science Research Council for the funds which made possible a stimulating experience. We thank the Duke University administration and the university library for the facilities provided. For assistance in launching this project, I am indebted to Paul H. Clyde, Professor of History and Director of the Summer Session; Joseph J. Spengler, James B. Duke Professor of Economics; R. Taylor Cole, James B. Duke Professor of Political Science; Professor Paul M. Gross, Vice-President of the University; Professor Alan K. Manchester, Dean of Trinity College, all of Duke University; and to Ray Allen Billington, William Mason Smith Professor of History, Northwestern University; and Richard W. Leopold, Professor of History, Northwestern University. For assistance in bringing the essays into print I am indebted and grateful to Professor John R. Alden, Department of History, Duke University and to Ashbel G. Brice, Director and Editor of Duke University Press.

ALEXANDER DECONDE

Durham, North Carolina
January 28, 1957

Introduction

INTERNATIONAL DIPLOMACY, used in its broad sense to include the mysterious processes through which nations and their governments devise foreign policies and the ideological assumptions from which these so-called policies are supposed to emerge, has not been a principal or a continuing preoccupation of the American people or, for that matter, of its government until very recent times. There was a period, to be sure, in early American experience when the specter of foreign affairs captured the public and the official eye and ear, but, with the passing of those early years, the direction of American interest turned inward rather than outward and it so remained until into the twentieth century.

Prior to 1900 there were two rather clearly defined periods in the American diplomatic experience. The first of these, encompassing the years from 1776 to 1823, was concerned with the achievement of independence, political and economic. It was a period when Americans were well versed in the vagaries of foreign policy. The great goal of independent nationhood was won by men who knew Europe as well as America. Out of their endeavors were born, along with the nation itself, the historic principles of American foreign policy: independence, the freedom of the seas, neutrality, nonintervention, commercial reciprocity under the conditional most-favored-nation formula, isolation, and the Monroe Doctrine. In the second period, the remainder of the nineteenth century, it seemed that the mere enunciation of these principles was the master key to diplomatic success. The world of Europe became less than a vital interest while the nation at home, all but untouched by foreign involvement, grew to fulness and strength. Foreign policy had already achieved its purposes. There were even suggestions that the diplomatic service might be done away with. There was little disposition to understand that the diplomatic success of the United States in the nineteenth century might not be due to abstract principles, no matter how right these principles might be, but rather to specific and definable circumstance: "the wars, rivalries, and distresses of Europe," the balance of power in the Old World at that time, the detached geographical position of the United States, remote from strong or aggressive neighbors, all of which left the American people at ease to pursue their interests at home in their own particular way, unhampered by foreign complexities.

At the turn of the twentieth century Americans could reflect, if they were so disposed, on a happy diplomatic record. The principles for which they believed they stood in foreign affairs could easily be defended as "good" principles. In their dealings with foreign powers successive American administrations, even without much calculation and certainly with less intrigue, had made few mistakes and had won substantial rewards. In the 1890's and after, some Americans at least could view the growth of the new and larger policy that was to carry the United States into world affairs with a confidence born of success. Yet within less than half a century this confidence, if not shattered, was certainly dimmed. The security and independence of the United States could no longer be taken for granted. The Freedom of the Seas was a memory. Neutrality and nonintervention had ceased to be virtues. The Monroe Doctrine had been altered beyond recognition, and the doctrine of isolation found the United States at the center of two World Wars. When in 1916 Americans re-elected a President because "He kept us out of war," they subscribed, doubtless without so intending, to a diplomatic revolution without precedent in the history of democratic government. Again, as in the days of the Founding Fathers, foreign policy had become a principal and continuing preoccupation of the American people and its government. Foreign relations ceased to be a polite diversion; they had become an unwelcome necessity. For the first time in nearly a century Americans were compelled to recognize that the world of foreign powers had moved in upon their domestic political privacy.

The response of Americans during the past forty years to this new involvement beyond the territorial limits of the United States has often appeared as a wild tumult of counsels; bewildering, extravagant, and unformed. Yet beneath this surface confusion had been solid strivings by responsible citizens, statesmen, and scholars to examine anew the principles that underlie American foreign policy, to discern its theoretical bases, to uncover the processes by which it has been formed, and to distinguish between its real and its imaginary content. The essays which follow in these pages are collectively at one and the same time a substantive contribution to this subject and an experiment in methodology.

Assisted by the Social Science Research Council, seven scholars in the disciplines of economics, history, and political science met for eight weeks at Duke University in the summer of 1956 as an interuniversity and interdisciplinary seminar to examine the nature and the place of the doctrines of isolation and of collective security in American diplomacy during the twentieth century. Each member of the seminar, though still young in years, had a substantial record of active research in American diplomacy, and each was already engaged on an individual specific project in research at the time he was invited to join the seminar. Each brought to the seminar a draft essay on his research to that point. During the subsequent sessions these essays were subjected to friendly, rigorous and, at points, devastating criticism. Under these repeated assaults each author dug deeper into the sources, subjected his evidence to re-evaluation, and labored with the science and art of putting thoughts into words. The essays that form this small but thoughtful volume are the result.

As contributions in economics, or in history, or in political science each essay can be said to stand on its own merits. However, having observed this summer seminar in operation, I am convinced that these merits (always acknowledging the individual capacities and skills of the authors) are derived in some notable measure from the unique character of the seminar itself as a pioneering venture in methodology. Operating without censor or arbiter, the seminar provided a means for a free interchange of ideas that could be and were often challenged from a plane of complete equality. The effectiveness of this interchange was increased further because the members of the seminar represented not one but a rather wide diversity of viewpoints on such matters as isolation and collective security. Here the group functioned not to impose conformity but to expose inadequate evidence, imperfect evaluation, or subjective judgment at variance with established data. In this mood this interdisciplinary seminar was in itself a laboratory on techniques and methods in three of the social sciences. There was the inescapable reminder that the economist, the historian, and the political scientist each uses and is dependent upon methods and techniques beyond those of his own discipline.

The basic subject with which the seminar was concerned, the conflict, real or supposed, between isolation and collective security, had not been treated previously in so comprehensive a manner. This book does not pretend to be exhaustive, but it does clarify the structure of the problems involved. It goes beyond the subject of diplomatic note-writing, beyond such generalities as nationalism and imperialism, to dissect, if this may be, the ideas from which foreign policy springs and to explore the philosophies that policy-makers have espoused. Here the seminar was cultivating new ground broken only recently.

Readers of these essays need hardly be reminded of the new and baffling role American diplomacy has been called upon to play in the twentieth century, of the vicious nature of some public debates on policy, of the tendency to find solutions in slogans, of the assumption that what is needed is more moralists or more realists according to the point of view, and of the widely held conviction that American moral principles as applied to foreign policy are universal moral principles. Certainly there can be no question that essays that dig beneath the surface of these symptoms merit our thoughtful attention. They remind us that the present generation of younger social scientists who see American diplomacy in the immediate context of two world wars are also aware of the larger and longer American experience from which our present successes and failures are derived. They bring into clearer perspective the ideas we have used and misused and the conclusions we have drawn from them.

PAUL H. CLYDE

Durham, North Carolina

Contents

Isolation
and
Security

1. *Alexander DeConde*

On Twentieth-Century Isolationism

We should, as the Second World War recedes into the distance, try—more conscientiously than we have done—to understand the motives and assumptions of those who described themselves as isolationists as well as the motives and assumptions of those who took a contrary view.
DEXTER PERKINS, 1956

SINCE THE FOUNDING of the Federal Republic in 1789 and through the nineteenth century the idea of political isolation from Europe has probably formed our most fundamental theory of foreign policy. Through that century of relative peace and into the strife-torn twentieth century Americans equated isolation, the desire to live their lives in peace and quiet and to work out their national destiny unhampered by foreign commitments, with patriotism. Isolation appeared to them to be a naturally ordained and permanent condition, and something distinctively American. It became an American tradition, a sacred legacy on the same lofty level as religion.

Americans were deeply conscious of isolation's historical roots; they associated isolation with the Founding Fathers and the heroes of the Revolution, particularly with George Washington. No administration in the nineteenth century dared depart from an isolationist policy, nor did any need to. Only in the twentieth century did statesmen seriously challenge isolation. Although a product of geographical circumstances and international politics which made possible aloofness from Europe, nineteenth-century isolation also stemmed from the idea that events in Europe could not injure the things Americans cherish.

Isolation through most of the nineteenth century was a doctrine of self-preservation, a broad idea of self-interest. There was little danger in that century that we would intervene in the affairs of Europe or that we would need European help. Our neighbors were weak; we were strong. The problem of American statesmen was not really to steer clear of European entanglements; it was to be vigilant and to prevent European intervention in our affairs. Europe's troubles made their task easy.

Americans—usually politicians, historians, and publicists—explained isolation as a desire to avoid involvement in the endless quarrels of Europe. We would not meddle in European affairs if Europeans would keep hands off our business. Expressed in this way the doctrine of isolation fed American pride. This was the talk of equals, satisfying to the ego of American nationalism. Out of this doctrine of self-preservation, buttressed by nationalism, grew twentieth-century isolationism.

But twentieth-century isolationism did not grow as one plant. Instead it became more than one thing. In the twentieth century we have actually had "isolationisms" rather than "isolationism." What Americans have called isolationism was a cluster of ideas and emotions related to isolation. It was also a variety of reactions to foreign policy. To different groups it meant different things. Isolationism fluctuated in strength and its basic assumptions differed according to the times, to the ideas, and to the motives of those who espoused it.

In the twentieth century the earlier isolation lost its sacred status as dogma and its position as fundamental policy. It became isolationism, one of several doctrines influencing American foreign policy. Statesmen no longer felt compelled to guide foreign policy by isolationist traditions. Beginning at the close of the nineteenth century statesmen and intellectuals like Theodore Roosevelt, John Hay, Alfred Thayer Mahan, Richard Olney, and others openly attacked traditional isolation as the basis for American foreign policy. Writing in 1898, Olney, a former Secretary of State, assailed the basic premise of nineteenth-century isolation, that it served national self-interest. "There is," he said, "a patriotism of race as well as of country"; we should abandon isolation for a policy of close co-operation with England. In the twentieth century, he warned, isolationism could be as dangerous as entanglement with Europe had been in the past.

As the twentieth century grew older, the opponents of isolationism grew in number. Intense opposition, among other things, distinguished the doctrines of isolationism from the isolation of the preceding century. In the eras of the First and Second World Wars highly placed statesmen, intellectuals, and others condemned isolationism as unpatriotic and un-American. In September, 1919, President Woodrow Wilson implied that only disloyal, pro-German Americans were organized in opposition to the Versailles Treaty. Twenty years later, in June 1940, Robert E. Sherwood, one of President Franklin D. Roosevelt's speech-writers, ran a full-page advertisement in several key newspapers calling for help to the allied nations fighting Hitler's Germany. "Will the Nazis considerately wait until we are ready to fight them?" he wrote. Then he lashed out at isolationists. "Anyone who argues that they will wait is either an imbecile or a traitor."

Americans had made an about-face. What had formerly been almost a touchstone of patriotism was now virtually disloyalty. Isolationists resented Sherwood's words. One of them, Oswald Garrison Villard, a former editor of the *Nation*, protested. Millions of Americans like himself, he said, might be wrong in their isolationist beliefs, but we are "just as loyal, just as sincere, and just as earnest Americans as Sherwood or anybody else."

By the Second World War so violently did Americans react to the issue of isolationism that the word *isolationism* became charged with derogatory meaning. To some it became a dirty word. Even those who professed what had formerly been the patriotic virtues of isolation shunned the label isolationist. They called their doctrines by other names such as "nationalism," "continentalism," or "Continental Americanism." "I was an isolationist, and I am a thousand times more isolationist today than I was before we became engaged in this war," wrote Senator Robert R. Reynolds of North Carolina, chairman of the Senate Military Affairs Committee, in July, 1943. "But that is my privilege.   However, I prefer to be referred to as an America Firster, or a Nationalist."

After the war isolationists, in most parts of the country, continued unpopular.   "How can we be isolationists," protested Senator Robert A. Taft, a leader of Midwestern isolationist sentiment, "when we are involved in wars and treaties and every kind of international relationship?"

What changed isolation from a "good and sensible" policy in the nineteenth century to a "bad" one in the twentieth? What, according to its opponents, made isolation as a policy and as an idea pernicious? Was the isolationism of the twentieth century based on the same conditions and the same ideas as that of the preceding century?   Whether different or the same as the earlier isolation, what was the ideological framework of the isolationism of the twentieth century?

I

While isolation as a doctrine has always been complex and made up of many ideas, the isolationist ideology of the nineteenth century was relatively simple when compared with that of the twentieth century. By stressing that their ideas were anchored in the revered past, isolationists of the present century identified them with Americanism and self-interest. To some they were nothing more than that. Yet twentieth-century isolationism was different from the isolation of the nineteenth.   It was different, we shall see, because it was a complex of emotions and ideas; because some of its ideas and vocabulary had changed; because the world of the nineteenth century was no more; and because the United States of the twentieth century was ethnically and culturally different from what it had been in the preceding century.

That the first vigorous critics of traditional isolation made themselves heard at the end of the nineteenth century and in the beginning of the twentieth was not accidental.   Their criticisms reflected changes in the world and in the United States. By the turn of the century the United States was a world power; a powerful Germany had forced Great Britain to abandon her "splendid isolation" by challenging her maritime and industrial supremacy; Great Britain began a new *rapprochement* with the United States, a *rapprochement* stronger than a formal alliance; and streams of "new immigrants" accelerated the change in the ethnic, social, and political composition of the United States started earlier by Germans and Irish. Externally and internally those developments changed or modified traditional American values. In particular they made isolationism different from the isolation of the past.

The world of the nineteenth century, in which American isolation was a political fact and served the nation well, was a world policed by the British fleet, a world in which Englishmen grew rich and Americans prospered peacefully. "America lives in a world of peace," wrote Lord Bryce of the nineteenth-century United States. "Safe from attack, safe even from menace, she hears from afar the warring cries of European nations and faiths. For the present at least—it may not always be so —America sails upon a summer sea." The summer sea became a storm-churned one because the balance of power in Europe, and in the world, shifted. This European balance of power Americans considered evil, an evil they shunned.

Our victory over Spain and the possession of the Philippines made us a weighty factor in the shifting power balance. We participated in European rivalries through the back of door of Asia. In Asia, too, Japan successfully challenged the old power status and the traditional hegemony of the Western World. Her victory over Russia in 1904-5 marked the beginning of the end of Europe's nineteenth-century dominance over colored peoples. In Europe, Germany challenged English pre-eminence, which for a century had commanded peace and stability. England responded by reversing her traditional diplomatic commitments on the Continent and by seeking an alliance or close understanding with the United States.

When Germany's challenge in the First World War almost succeeded in destroying the English-dominated and French-supported *status quo*, it changed the thinking of many Americans on foreign policy, particularly on isolationism. Even in defeat Germany had destroyed the old balance of power. England was no longer the balancer; the United States was.

Many Americans wedded to the ideas of nineteenth-century isolation now realized, as perhaps they had not before, that they had profited from England's manipulation of the balance of power. The things they considered important and wished to preserve, Germany endangered. Woodrow Wilson stressed this when he urged the nation on that fateful April 2, 1917, "to spend her blood and her might for the principles that gave her birth and happiness and the peace that she has treasured."

Americans held most of those principles, political, institutional, social, and cultural, in common with England, and France shared some of them. Essentially, their peaceful enjoyment had rested on England's maritime and diplomatic ascendancy in the nineteenth century. To preserve these common institutions and ideals when England seemed no longer capable of holding a commanding influence in world politics, or even of maintaining the nineteeth-century equilibrium, many Americans had urged participation in the First World War and rejoiced when we entered it. They forsook the traditional principles of isolationism and saw with satisfaction that American intervention tipped the balance in favor of France and England.

But the balance of power was not the same; the old nineteenth-century detachment of the United States could not be regained. America had become the decisive weight in the balance. As Theodore Roosevelt had told a German friend before the war (1911), the United States, because of its geographical position and great strength, was becoming more and more the most important power in the world's balance of power. Yet even after the World War most Americans persisted in thinking that the balance of power was evil and should be shunned. Cordell Hull, an internationalist Secretary of State who favored participation in world politics, was, if not typical, at least representative of this kind of thinking. He never believed in the balance of power as a means of keeping the peace. During the First World War, he explained in his memoirs, he studied the balance of power and was convinced it was iniquitous. "The conclusions I then formed in total opposition to this system," he said, "stayed with me."

When after the war the victors established a world organization predicated on maintaining the *status quo* of the wartime Allied coalition it failed. The League of Nations failed, many Americans reasoned, because the United States, the fulcrum in the new balance of power, would not participate in collective action to uphold the balance. For reasons germane more to internal developments than to international affairs the United States tried to slip back into the comfortable isolation of the past. Actually, while the words and some of the ideas sounded the same, isolationism too had changed.

It was no longer a doctrine of self-preservation on which almost all Americans agreed. Opponents argued that it was the unthinking defensive posture of the ostrich; it did not fit the facts of international affairs in the twentieth century. The true doctrine of self-preservation, they argued, was collective security. While agreeing that the world and America's relationships with other nations had changed, isolationists contended that their doctrine was still best for self-preservation. In the 1920's and 1930's most Americans seemed to agree.

In less than two decades after the First World War Germany again challenged the international *status quo*. This time Japan and Italy were also challengers. Again the United States entered the war to tip the balance in favor of England; again Americans, more of them than in 1917, believed ultimately that American intervention was essential to preserve important Anglo-American values.

When the United States entered the Second World War it did not do so as an outsider interested primarily in preserving the dominant status of a close friend with the idea of returning home after the peace and leaving the friend once more responsible for the balance of power. This time, as had not been clearly the case in the First World War, the challenge to the upholders of the established balance threatened American security.

Although England for a while held off Germany alone, the United States, not she, became the main defender of the old international *status quo*. At the same time a new and powerful ally, Soviet Russia, helped destroy the German-Japanese challenge. But Communist Russia did not value the ideals Americans, Englishmen, and Frenchmen shared.

With the end of the Second World War a newly polarized distribution of power emerged. At one end was Russia, determined to destroy what remained of the old international *status quo*. At the other pole was the United States, a firm opponent of Communist power but a reluctant defender of remnants of England's nineteenth-century world hegemony. Whether or not most Americans liked it, the United States had inherited Great Britain's role as the pivot of the Western World; it became the main defender of Anglo-American values. America's security, particularly after Russia had penetrated the secret of the atom, was now linked with that of Europe and of all the world. Not even a Procrustes could force those facts to fit the doctrine of nineteenth-century isolation.

II

Actually twentieth-century isolationists did not try to force century-old ideas on the new facts of their time. They modified some of their ideas to fit the new circumstances but they came out with nineteenth-century conclusions. One reason for this was that isolationism had most of the trappings of the old isolation even though it grew as much from the internal changes paralleling the changes in international relations as it did from historic traditions.

The new isolationists insisted, as had the old, that Europe was a source of trouble, hatreds, alliances, strange "isms," and wars. Her troubles in the twentieth as in the nineteenth century did not concern the United States. We should mind our own business, said the new isolationists, echoing a familiar refrain, and not get involved in her endless quarrels. "We ask only to live our own life in our own way," said California's Senator Hiram Johnson in March, 1922, "in friendship and sympathy with all, in alliance with none." As late as October, 1935, President Franklin D. Roosevelt expressed similar sentiments. In San Diego, California, he said that "despite what happens in continents overseas, the United States of America shall and must remain, as long ago the Father of our Country prayed that it might remain—unentangled and free."

This espousal of traditional isolationist dogma was popular because all Americans shared the nineteenth-century heritage and most of them, to a degree at least, valued traditions commonly associated with isolation. Most Americans hated war and militarism; an important element in the old isolation was detestation of Europe's military strife. The antimilitarism carried over into isolationism. Parents who had never known military service and those who had known it, perhaps in Europe, shrank from the thought that their sons might be mangled or slain on foreign battle fields for issues seemingly alien and remote.

Those fearful mothers and fathers supported isolationism, and their support reflected the antimilitarist element which was prominent in the isolationism of the 1920's and 1930's and carried to the Second World War. In April, 1948, just five months before he died, Charles A. Beard, considered by many the intellectual leader of isolationism, addressed a statement to the Armed Forces Services Committee of the Senate denouncing militarism as a violation of American tradition. "Universal military training, so-called," he said, "represents an attempt to implant in the United States a well-known curse of the Old World."

Other Americans, oftentimes extreme nationalists, were isolationists because they distrusted foreigners, a not unusual sentiment among all peoples. Some Americans were chronic British-haters. In the twentieth century they formed a hard core of the isolationist movement. As much as anything else they gave the isolationism of the twentieth century a distinctive characteristic marking it off from the past. One reason for this was that the basically British composition of the population had changed. The change brought conflicting Old World loyalties to the United States, loyalties reflected in politics and foreign policy.

Many of the newer Americans of the twentieth century did not place the same values on traditional isolationist dogma as did the older British-stock Americans. Yet many of the new Americans, as well as those older ones of Irish and German origins who had started coming in the nineteenth century and had attained political influence by the opening of the twentieth, were stanch isolationists. Their isolationism was based on an ethnic reaction to American foreign policy and on blood and cultural ties to the Old World. "Every man loves his native land," an Irishman once aptly said, "whether he was born there or not." Many of these new isolationists had little more in common than an innate antipathy to anything English. But this was strong enough to make some of them extreme nationalists, the new standard-bearers of traditional isolationist philosophy.

After the Spanish-American War the main argument against foreign commitments and internationalism was the historical tradition of isolation with all that it implied. But already the ethnic element showed that traditional isolation had changed. Irish-Americans denounced the *rapprochement* with England preached by such men as John Hay; and German-Americans joined them. Finley Peter Dunne ("Mr. Dooley"), for example, swore to do all within his power to stem the tide of friendly co-operation with England.

German-Americans supported isolationism as a form of Anglophobia and as a means of expressing their indignation over the Boer War. So strong was this ethnic isolationism combined with traditional isolationist ideas that anglophile John Hay did not dare present his Open Door notes to the American people as coming from Anglo-American sources. He presented them, and the international principle they involved, as being purely American.

Other immigrant groups brought Old World loyalties with them also; some brought anti-British proclivities. But as a class they were usually at the bottom of the social, economic, and political scale; they could do little about foreign policy until they gained political influence. When the First World War broke out it aroused ethnic isolationism as it had not been aroused before. It also revived the old isolationist dogmas and created new arguments. Again Irish-Americans and German-Americans formed the backbone of isolationism.

Noting that the Midwest was the most isolationist section of the country, some students of isolationism concluded that geographical insularity and ignorance of international affairs were the sources of isolationism. Actually ethnic concentration offered a better explanation for Midwestern isolationism. The Midwest was heavily populated by German-Americans and by Scandinavian-Americans who in the First World War were isolationist and pro-German. They had attained political power; they largely determined the section's political reaction to American foreign policy, particularly to events in Europe.

Although isolationism in the First World War had an ideological foundation, it was also a complex of emotions based on cultural and ethnic ties. The same was true of internationalism. Those who wanted the United States to intervene in the war were also moved by ethnic and cultural emotions. Their leaders were often Anglophiles or men who placed salvation of England almost on the same plane as defense of the United States. When President Wilson denounced hyphenate groups as unpatriotic and un-American he appeared to many of the newer Americans not as an unbiased national leader but as the spokesman of the most powerful hyphenate group of all, the Anglo-Americans. Reacting to foreign policy in the same manner as any other ethnic strain, they demanded and won support for the "mother country."

Interventionists in the First World War pointed out that the values Americans cherished most could no longer be protected by a policy of isolation. They pointed out again and again, as did English propagandists and as had Olney earlier, that they were values held in common with England and that German militarism endangered them. Writing in November, 1941, David Lewis Einstein, historian and diplomat, contended that

America's relative isolation did not depend on geography but on the survival of British sea power and the old balance of power. A German victory, he argued, would endanger American security. To prevent this, he said, "We must extend the Monroe Doctrine to England, and embrace the foremost American power after our own." He argued in terms of self-preservation, the essence of traditional isolationist theory. In effect he maintained that traditional isolation included England; that it was really a form of limited internationalism.

The idea of shared Anglo-American values was common on both sides of the water. When the United States finally entered the war, members of England's Council of the Royal Historical Society declared "their satisfaction that the alliance . . . has now been completed, and that all sections of the Anglo-British race are now arrayed side by side in defense of the historic liberties common to them all."

Like the pro-German hyphenates, intellectuals and other leaders in American life, when they attacked isolationism, were moved by blood and cultural ties with England. Historians, among others, tried to effect a friendlier interpretation of Anglo-American history by emphasizing the English origins of American ideals and institutions. School textbooks, in new revisions, reflected the Anglo-American unity.

Professor William T. Hutchinson of the University of Chicago surveyed a number of articles by American historians emphasizing common Anglo-American origin. He wrote that from their writings "the conclusion is inescapable that the American people are almost exclusively English in ancestry [and that] other immigrant groups have contributed little if anything to America's heritage of liberalism." Hutchinson found that at least five scholars, probably working independently, reached the identical conclusion "that Wilson's internationalism and Monroe's isolationism were in complete accord." Both men, they said, were defending the same American ideals. What they tried to show was that intervention in behalf of England, rather than isolationism, had now become a criterion of patriotism.

George B. Adams, another historian, tried to show that basically "England is not a foreign nation." He wrote in 1918 that "the war has taught us . . . the people of America and the people of the British Empire are so nearly alike in their fundamental political ideas, aims and institutions, in their attitude towards questions of foreign relations . . . that a common policy in relation to all the rest of the world would be as easily formed between them, and as easily conducted, as between New York and Iowa, or any two of our states."

In the First World War many interventionists and isolationists actually approached foreign policy with similarly aroused emotions. They differed primarily in the sides they preferred. What this meant for the isolationists was that they were not indifferent to Europe's wars and politics. They were as sensitive to foreign affairs as were the internationalists, and governed their attitudes toward American foreign policy by their emotional responses to European situations.

Isolationists in most instances were not less loyal than interventionists. Their sentiments, however, were usually exploited by opposition political parties and sometimes by demagogues. In the view of the ethnic isolationist the truly patriotic foreign policy would be an isolationist foreign policy, but not essentially because it would shun Europe's wars. He favored an isolationist foreign policy because it would not be so directed as to make an enemy of the land of his origin.

The ethnic isolationists, as well as other isolationists, did not consistently oppose intervention in Asia. Many of them in later years supported a leadership favoring intervention in the Far East while opposing it in Europe. In the Midwest they read Colonel Robert R. McCormick's Chicago *Tribune* and in other parts of the country they read the papers of William Randolph Hearst, which emphasized constantly that the "yellow peril" was the main threat to American national interests. One reason for this paradoxical isolationist attitude toward Europe coupled with belligerent alarm over events in Asia was that a strong policy in the Far East did not involve co-operation with England, as did intervention in Europe.

Another reason was probably the fact that the United States contained no important ethnic group of Asian origin capable of influencing politics.

More than the Midwest was isolationist, the South was traditionally internationalist. Again the cultural and ethnic affinities of its people explained its reaction to foreign policy better than adherence to any theory or philosophy of foreign relations. In large measure English or Scottish in background, the South had attracted few of the new immigrants or of the older non-Anglo-Saxon immigrants. It had no European, particularly no German or Irish, tradition. Actually, it was not so much internationalist in viewpoint as it was pro-English. Without significant numbers of European immigrants, the South did not suffer divided emotional allegiances. It was as solid in its attachment to a pro-English foreign policy in time of crisis as it was in its traditional attachment to the Democratic party. In the two World Wars, moreover, the South did not have an opposition party capable of exploiting whatever isolationist sentiment it might have.

The East, with its heavy concentration of new immigrants fused to an English cultural tradition, was generally most sensitive to European affairs. But this sensitivity did not make it as consistently internationalist in sentiment as the South. Depending on the nature of European quarrels, many of the newer Americans became isolationists and not internationalists because of their intense interest in European affairs. Those of Irish, German, and Italian origins are good examples. Sometimes opposing ethnic allegiances to Europe tended to cancel each other as political forces.

In the Second World War the same general pattern of cultural and ethnic isolationism as in the last war repeated itself. In the period between the wars the new immigrants and their offspring acquired a higher social and economic status, but, more important, they acquired political power. More than in the First World War Catholicism and isolationism appeared closely linked. One reason for this was the increased influence in American life on the part of Catholics who were led by an

Irish-dominated church hierarchy unwilling to forget anti-British grievances. Too, the pattern of cultural and ethnic isolationism became tangled. Polish-Americans, Jewish-Americans, and the formerly pro-German Norwegian and Danish-Americans were now fiercely anti-German. They now believed that the ideals they cherished could be protected only in an Anglo-American alliance. They were interventionist and anti-isolationist.

Even among anti-British isolationists of German and Irish ancestry, kinship with the land of origin was often not sufficient to overcome loathing for Adolf Hitler. Yet these groups still formed the hard core of isolationist sentiment. They were supported by some Italian-Americans who remembered Italian frustrations at the peace conference after the First World War and who resented President Roosevelt's humiliating condemnation of Benito Mussolini's attack on France, and by some Swedish-Americans who felt a kinship with a Germany then at war with Russia, Sweden's traditional enemy. The distinctive anti-English bias in the new isolationism was persistent. In 1922 Secretary of State Charles E. Hughes had to deny isolationist Senator William E. Borah's charge that the Washington Conference had brought about an alliance or secret understanding with England. Similarly in the late 1930's isolationists repeatedly forced President Roosevelt to deny that the State Department had a secret understanding or alliance with England.

III

Another element in the complex of twentieth-century isolationism was economic and social reform. The First World War ended the Progressive Era. At that time the tide of public sentiment ran against monopolies, "Wall Street," and the "money trust." Reformers demanded economic and social reforms in government; many of them believed England was the center of the international "money power." They joined forces with isolationists who opposed internationalism for other reasons. The liberal isolationists justified their opposition to intervention by arguing it stifled reform at home, and by applying an economic interpretation to the war which reduced it "to a blood-spattered grab for profit."

President Woodrow Wilson at first appeared to be a champion of the liberal reformers, particularly before the war when he denounced dollar diplomacy and the use of foreign policy to advance the power of vested interests. He changed, but the liberal reformers did not. They insisted that the "selfish" vested interests sought to lead the nation to war as a means of aborting reform.

Some of the reformers combined economic isolationism with ethnic isolationism. During the First World War a Swedish immigrant and a leading isolationist, Charles A. Lindbergh, Sr., did this in a book, *Why Is Your Country at War and What Happens to You after the War, and Related Subjects* (1917), a book government agents suppressed. In it he blamed the war on profiteers and international bankers.

After the war the liberals insisted that domestic reform was a substitute for diplomacy. Those liberal isolationists adopted John Maynard Keynes's *The Economic Consequences of the Peace* (1919) as their bible. From Keynes's disillusioning anti-treaty arguments the liberals formed an ideological justification for isolationism which the ethnic isolationists adopted. Between the two World Wars reformers like John Dewey, Thorstein Veblen, and others preached that the League of Nations was corrupt and imperialistic and that Woodrow Wilson had betrayed liberalism.

Economic reformers in the New Deal, which at first was basically isolationist, advanced similar views. Stuart Chase, among others, argued that intervention in 1917 caused economic dislocation and postponement of economic reform, and that America now should avoid unnecessary entanglement abroad and concentrate on solving social and economic problems at home.

Beard shared a similar view. He advanced the idea that internationalism was a program of escape from economic crisis. He concluded that economic pressures, among other causes, pulled the United States into the First World War. As the

Second World War approached and President Roosevelt shifted his main attention from domestic affairs to foreign affairs, Beard attributed the shift to Roosevelt's failure to solve America's economic crisis by purely national means.

This affinity of economic reformers for isolationism grew out of the belief that the war had betrayed their cause. The anti-liberal hysteria of the 1920's probably strengthened this feeling. Many progressives also nurtured the general attitude that to be concerned with foreign affairs was to neglect unsolved problems at home. William E. Borah, Hiram Johnson, George W. Norris, and other isolationist-liberals of the 1920's favored government intervention at home but opposed all intervention abroad. Even Franklin D. Roosevelt took a similar view at first; he went into office with considerable support for his domestic New Deal program from isolationist progressives.

Liberal economic isolationism reached a climax in 1934 with Senator Gerald P. Nye's investigation of the munitions industry. He contended that foreign loans and munitions profits dragged the United States into the First World War. Disillusioned by the results of the war, by the failure of Wilsonian idealism, and holding bankers in low esteem in those depression years, the public was ready to believe the worst of "greedy businessmen." That war profiteers, "merchants of death," had tricked the nation into war became a popular dogma. The public hailed Nye's thesis, long popular with the liberal isolationists, as a sensational revelation of suppressed truth.

Nye's charge merged with the always strong antiwar sentiment, which now found support for its bitter memories of intervention in the last war. Participation in the First World War was a mistake, isolationists reasoned; the Nye investigation and events since had showed that it was; traditional isolationist policy still served America's self-interest best. This feeling influenced many at the time. Harry S. Truman, for example, voted for the Neutrality Act of 1937 in the Senate because he did not want the United States to become involved in the Spanish Civil War. "I was misled by the report of the munitions investigation which was led by Gerald Nye," he wrote in his memoirs.

The Second World War shattered the liberal pattern of isolationism which had carried into the interwar period and reached a peak in the 1930's. When war came a new, economically motivated pattern of isolationism had emerged. Although the isolationist movement of the Second World War included men of diverse economic and social philosophies, and even some of the old economic reformers, at that time conservative business interests formed the leadership of the movement as a reaction against Franklin D. Roosevelt's New Deal. Most of these leaders, who provided the rationale, the ideas, and the funds for the new isolationism, were conservative Republicans. These conservative business leaders formed the backbone of the America First movement prior to the Second World War, the strongest isolationist organization in the country. But not all conservatives and not all big businessmen were isolationists; many, particularly in the East, supported Roosevelt's foreign policy.

In direct contrast to the liberal isolationists of the 1914-1917 period, who justified their opposition to war by arguing that intervention snuffed out reform at home, conservative isolationists in the period of the Second World War attacked the Roosevelt administration's internationalism as a disguised effort to force social reform on the nation. Isolationist leadership, preoccupied with opposition to the New Deal, had gone to the right economically.

The Second World War split the economic reformers of the left from their alliance with the isolationists. Even though there were notable exceptions, the economic liberals moved into or stayed with the Democratic party and supported intervention. The isolationists, now allied with conservative economic leaders, either moved into or stayed with the Republican party. Many America First leaders believed American entrance into the war would bring national bankruptcy and the collapse of the American system of capitalism and free enterprise.

Whether liberal or conservative, economically founded isolationism in the twentieth century was not a constant force. It changed with the economic situation. Although its principles seemed traditional, the arguments supporting them were not. The economic attitudes of the isolationists themselves also differed according to the times and to the men in power.

Despite the fluctuations in economic isolationism, as in cultural, ethnic, and social isolationism, the isolationists of the Second World War period generally repeated the arguments and theories of 1914-1917. Isolationists of the 1930's believed that American intervention in the first World War had been a tragedy; there should not be a second such tragedy. They were convinced the same mistake could be avoided if the Roosevelt administration protected the people with wise laws reflecting traditional isolationist theory. The neutrality legislation of the 1930's embodied their ideas and reflected their popular influence.

IV

Although nationalism has been a persistent strain in the history of American isolationism and prior to the Second World War was connected more with conservative than with any other leadership, it also attracted some of the liberals and intellectual idealists. These intellectual liberals, whose ideals were usually broad and international, ironically oftentimes supplied the arguments for a narrow isolationism and an ultranationalism. Actually the idealistic liberals had little in common with the conservative isolationist leadership other than a fear of war.

These liberal intellectual isolationists, such as Stuart Chase and Harry Elmer Barnes, did not deny the predominantly negative features of their isolationism but, they insisted, they also offered a positive doctrine. Again, as in so many instances, Beard was one of their clearest spokesmen. He defined isolationism many times, but a definition offered in 1946 is as clear as any. While giving high status to the usual negative principles of nonentanglement, nonintervention, and avoidance of war, he stressed the positive view that American foreign policy should be friendly to all nations willing to respond in the same way. Then he added an antiforce proviso combining the positive with the negative. "An isolationist," he said, "may favor promotion of good-will and peace among nations by any and all measures compatible with nonentanglement in any association of nations empowered to designate 'aggressors' and bring engines of sanction and coercion into action against them."

Beard, in his definition, also spoke for the idealistic isolationist who earlier had opposed the League of Nations. The liberal isolationist had opposed the League not for political reasons, as had many Republicans, but because he believed it entangled the United States in European politics and committed the nation to a policy of force to uphold a vindictive peace and a foreign *status quo*. Back in May, 1919, immediately after promulgation of the terms of the Versailles treaty, the *New Republic* in a cover-page statement had clearly expressed liberal disappointment with the peace. "Americans would be fools," it said, "if they permitted themselves to be embroiled in a system of European alliances. America promised to underwrite a stable peace. Mr. Wilson has failed. The peace cannot last. America should withdraw from all commitments which would impair her freedom of action."

This idealistic liberal reaction against the peace and the League also found support among the historical revisionists who wrote on both World Wars. They often advanced cogent arguments in support of the liberal idealistic isolationist position. Although giving the appearance of being rational and objective in their assessments, they too responded emotionally to the idea that peace depended on force. Actually they appeared more emotional in their isolationist views than did the conservative nationalists who based their isolationism almost wholly on self-interest and their own economic welfare.

v

Many of the intellectual isolationists of the two World Wars were pacifists who opposed any kind of foreign war, whether reactionary, liberal, international, or revolutionary. They would support only a war of self-defense. William Jennings Bryan, for example, was a pacifist-minded politician who resigned the Secretaryship of State rather than lead the nation into war. He considered militarism and popular government incompatible. His views were important not because of any originality, but because millions of Americans shared his pacifism and hatred of war. Yet millions of other Americans denounced him as pro-German for refusing to desert principles long associated with traditional isolation. Bryan believed war strengthened militarism, enriched the industrial and financial classes he had always fought, and diverted attention from the domestic problems he believed the nation should solve. In his thinking he combined pacifism with economic liberalism to exemplify a fusion of these elements in isolationist thinking.

A distinguishing characteristic of liberal isolationists—indeed of all isolationists, but especially of many pacifists—in the 1930's was that they believed that wars in Europe and Asia did not seriously endanger the United States. They advanced the theory of American impregnability harking back to the old geographical basis of early isolation. "Not until some formidable European power comes into the western Atlantic, breathing the fire of aggression and conquest," wrote Beard in 1939, "need the United States become alarmed about the ups and downs of European conflicts, intrigues, aggressions, and wars." Beard, who was a liberal isolationist but not a pacifist, indicated clearly that he based his ideas on the traditional view of isolation as a doctrine of self-defense as promoted by George Washington.

Other isolationists, such as Oswald Garrison Villard, believed the United States was beyond danger of attack through the air, on the surface of the water, or below it. Even after war broke out in Europe he persisted in his view. "Actually, from the military point of view," he wrote in September, 1939, "the security of the United States has been increased by the outbreak of war. And the longer war continues, the safer the United States will be, if it ever was in danger. For with each day the exhaustion of the contestants will become greater."

Closely allied to the theory of impregnability, and at times almost indistinguishable from it, was the isolationism of power and preparedness, or the fortress concept of American security. The America First Committee expressed this theory succinctly in the original announcement of its principles.

1. The United states must build an impregnable defense for America.
2. No foreign power, nor group of powers, can successfully attack a *prepared* America.
3. American democracy can be preserved only by keeping out of the European war.

The fortress theory assumed that the United States, without powerful historic enemies north or south, was an impregnable fortress protected by two gigantic moats, a fortress manned by warriors capable of repelling any attack if it should come. With its emphasis on force this idea was the antithesis of pacifism and the liberal isolationism associated with it. Its strongest advocates were the conservative isolationists, men who did not feel obliged to disguise their appeal to individualistic nationalism with idealistic professions. They did not want to isolate America from Europe's troubles for the welfare of humanity or to spur economic reform; they wanted to do business as usual in a free enterprise system fed by a nationalism which would not subordinate America's freedom of action to the will of other nations. They based their isolationist arguments on military power and national self-interest. Some of their thinking was colored by traditional hatred of foreigners. This accounted for some of their popular following.

Former President Herbert Hoover, Senators Robert A. Taft and Arthur H. Vandenberg, and Charles A. Lindbergh, Jr., were among those who advanced the theory of the isolationism of power. Although these men did not frame their arguments in terms of Anglophobia or antiforeignism, their followers accepted their arguments as pointing to such a conclusion. These men differed from most liberals, interventionists, and isolationists, in that they argued in terms of cold self-interest. Some interventionists, however, argued in the same terms.

Basically those hard-headed isolationists believed national self-preservation depended solely on America's own defensive power protecting the Western Hemisphere and not on the British navy or the European balance of power. Even if Europe, and England with her navy, fell to Hitler, they argued, America could survive behind her impregnable fortress walls. Ambassador to England Joseph P. Kennedy urged Americans to reinforce their own position so that they could withstand the shock of Europe's fall.

Herbert Hoover expressed the theory perhaps as neatly as anyone. The United States, he stressed, was too strong to be defeated; its defense did not depend on any other nation. The Western Hemisphere, he said in February, 1939, was protected by a "moat of three thousand miles of ocean on the east, and six thousand miles on the west," all of which formed a virtually insurmountable military barrier. During the Korean War he emphasized the same idea. "The foundation of our national policies," he said in December, 1950, "must be to preserve for the world this Western Hemisphere Gibraltar of Western Civilization."

VI

What about isolationism after the Second World War? Did it exist, or was it, as Harry S. Truman told Franklin D. Roosevelt on the latter's election to his fourth term, dead? If it were alive was it any different from past isolationism? What were its common characteristics?

Isolationism still existed in the 1940's and the 1950's but it differed from that of the prewar decades. As Adlai E. Stevenson wrote in 1949, the "old fashioned" isolationism was moribund but there was a "reincarnation of its spirit." Instead of opposing involvement in war or membership in international organizations, it flowed into other channels. Pacifists, anti-militarists, xenophobes, Anglophobes, and others were still in existence, but they did not constitute an integrated and influential body of opinion. Even the old strategic arguments of Herbert Hoover and Robert A. Taft, calling for a fortress America, did not arouse a large following. In this era the United States became the center of a web of alliances. Stevenson called postwar isolationism "neo-isolation—international cooperation by elocution." He believed many people were "internationally minded in principle but not in practice"; that they favored "international cooperation in the abstract while opposing concrete steps to make it effective."

What bound isolationists together in this period was kindred emotions, the memory of opposition to the last war, and anti-Communism. But in the postwar world of the 1940's and 1950's isolationism had practically disappeared. Isolationists, for political and economic reasons, were still concentrated mostly in the Republican party. Still thinking in the past, they played on the emotional frustrations of the Cold War and the Korean War and asserted that the frustrations emanated from the alleged mistakes of the last war and from treason in high places. They attacked what they called the blunders of Yalta and Potsdam and blamed the victories of Communism on Roosevelt's conduct of the war. Senator Taft summarized this feeling in 1951 by pointing out that "our leaders failed to foresee that the Soviet Union would turn against us after the defeat of Germany and Japan. They made no attempt to insure our future against that eventuality."

As clearly as can be found elsewhere, the writings of the historical revisionists synthesized certain main ideas of the postwar isolationists. They raked over the causes and results of the war in trying to prove that the isolationists of the interwar period were right. By joining the fight in the Second World War, they argued, we made a serious mistake. Had we refused to fight, Russia would have lost and we would not be menaced by Soviet power.

Some of these newest isolationists found support in Catholic memories of the Spanish Civil War. In the high tide of anti-Communism, in fact, many Catholics felt postwar events proved that Communism and not liberal democracy had been crushed in Spain.   Then there were the usual fringe elements who always flocked to the isolationist banner, the xenophobes, anti-Semites, and others.   But the core of the newest isolationism was anti-Communism, primarily fear of Communist penetration from within the country.

Since the Russian Revolution of 1917 isolationists, particularly Catholics and economic conservatives, had tended to be anti-Russian.   Many of them had always maintained that Russia was the real enemy.   When Hitler attacked Russia, isolationists hoped that Germany and Russia would destroy each other. Hearst, who had been an isolationist in the First World War as in the second, opposed aid to Russia, arguing that Communists would be the eventual victors.

After we entered the war, and became in fact Russia's ally, isolationists favored concentrating the military effort against Japan instead of trying to beat Hitler first.   Hearst in his newspaper columns actually narrowed the war to a struggle between the Hearst empire and the Japanese empire.   During the war General Douglas MacArthur became the symbol of the beat-Japan-first movement and, after the war, of the Asia-first movement.   Those movements attracted considerable support from the old isolationists.

The fact that in the late 1940's Germany changed from an enemy to a potential ally and Russia from friend to foe undoubtedly strengthened the feeling among isolationists that Russia had been "the real enemy all along."   The Communist victory in China also probably bolstered their sense of vindication.   We should have saved China, they argued.   Democratic blundering lost it.

Just as America's emergence as a world power at the end of the nineteenth century, coupled with the destruction of the old balance of power, destroyed nineteenth-century isolation, the Russian-American power struggle virtually destroyed the ethnic foundations of twentieth-century isolationism.   Soviet imperialism forced the various national strains in the United States into a kind of unity in support of an anti-Russian foreign policy; former isolationists and interventionists were now on the same side. The stanchly Catholic and traditionally isolationist Irish-Americans, for example, now supported an anti-Russian foreign policy. The Russian and Chinese opponents of the American-led Western coalition had no support from large ethnic minorities in the United States which could form a nucleus for a new isolationism.

Opponents of the anti-Communist foreign policy might, however, build an isolationist movement on a foundation of nineteenth-century ideas, economic (class) cleavages, and Communist ideology. Some of these pro-Communist isolationists and others in 1948 did flock to the banner of Henry A. Wallace's Progressive party. Wallace had great appeal for reformers and the underprivileged; he spoke the universal language of peace. "The thing which disturbs me most about the United States," he said in 1948, " is the thing that also disturbs me most about the world—the dominance of faith in force as the ultimate arbiter." The atom bomb, he stressed, had made such a faith obsolete. To the war-weary and disillusioned, who foresaw a third world war and lived in fear of being reduced to radioactive fossils, Wallace's passionate belief in peace evoked admiration.

Yet when Wallace spoke as an internationalist and a believer in peace, he really spoke as a reformer-isolationist in a new context. He and his followers wanted the United States to stay out of European and Asiatic affairs; they wanted disarmament; and they attacked the Cold War with the traditional economic interpretation of the liberal isolationist. This time the liberals did not embrace a new pro-Russian isolationism. Even some of the narrower liberal isolationists had by mid-century become internationalists. As a one-time liberal isolationist professor remarked in August, 1950, "I have become an unwilling internationalist, but an internationalist nevertheless."

The conservative isolationist also, even though he embraced the anti-Russian crusade of the postwar era, was not satisfied with American foreign policy. He preferred a less international and a more nationalistic crusade. He still clutched at the idea that an isolated America could live securely without allies.

Senator Taft, even though he denied being an "isolationist," represented this view.

When President Harry S. Truman announced his Truman Doctrine to Congress in March, 1947, he actually used the unilateral approach espoused by the conservative isolationist. "We cannot allow changes in the status quo in violation of the Charter of the United Nations," he said, "by such methods as coercion, or by such subterfuges as political infiltration." For the first time while the nation was at peace, an American government committed itself to use force against another nation, and to do so unilaterally if necessary. Yet, at the time, isolationists of the right and left opposed the unilateral commitment. Later, the conservative isolationists accepted the commitment to force even though it destroyed a basic antiforce element of the older isolationism.

The change was noteworthy in Taft's reaction to the North Atlantic Treaty of April, 1949. He led the unsuccessful Senate fight to block it. Ironically, while he and the conservative isolationists led the legislative attack against the twelve-power alliance, the extreme left (Communists), plus the Wallace progressives, as pro-Russian isolationists, offered the loudest opposition. Yet Taft attacked the treaty as an anti-Russian isolationist and spoke the language of nationalism and tradition.

In a prepared interview in July, 1949, Taft explained his opposition. Instead of the multilateral North Atlantic Treaty he preferred a Monroe Doctrine type, or unilateral, declaration against Russia. "If a declaration of intent were made by the United States alone," he said, "we could withdraw from it when we wished to, on proper notice. This treaty binds us for twenty years. Under a Monroe Doctrine declaration we could decide, in each case, whether the attack was justified or not. Now we have to go to war, even if one of our allies has in some way instigated the attack." The conservative isolationist of the 1940's and 1950's, as Taft indicated, would use force to maintain the international *status quo* against Communism; but he wanted to do it alone. The internationalist would also use force to uphold the new *status quo* against Communism; but he wanted to do it collectively.

If not a complete repudiation of isolationism as some proponents claimed, the North Atlantic alliance certainly demolished the political strength of the antiforce and anti-entanglement principles. It also defied the anti-British tradition of isolationism; we had become official partners of Great Britain. Now that England was no longer a foremost world power we were committed to maintain the international *status quo* of the Western World as she had in the nineteenth century with her *Pax Britannica*. We now headed a new balance of power in a *Pax Atlantica*.

VII

While isolationism in the twentieth century as a theory of foreign relations was usually negative and inconsistent, it had certain positive features which were always evident in a fairly consistent pattern. Like many theories of political conduct, its most appealing and therefore most persistent feature was utopian. Isolation or immunity from trouble is an ideal almost all peoples at one time or another have aspired to achieve. For some it represented an ideal as blissful as the Buddhist Nirvana.

For this reason, if for no other, at mid-century isolationism in one form or another still lived. It still had political attractions. Those attractions could be seen as late as February, 1954, in the fight over the Bricker Amendment to the Constitution, an amendment designed to give Congress decisive power over treaties and executive agreements. So strongly did the isolationist-minded rally behind the amendment, in spite of President Dwight D. Eisenhower's opposition, that it failed by only one vote to receive the necessary two-thirds support in the Senate.

Yet isolationists again met defeat. In spite of his utopian ideal the twentieth-century isolationist met nothing but frustration. His utopia seemed in the past rather than in the future. Tradition formed its main bulwark.

Another consistent quality in isolationism, closely allied to the ideal of shunning trouble, was the universal desire to avoid war. To many Americans isolationism was nothing more than isolation from war. Although manifested in diverse ways, such as antimilitarism, this antiwar element ran through all forms of isolationist dogma, either as an idea or an emotion. Most often this antiwar concept in isolationism was a direct response to American foreign policy in a specific context, and usually it was linked with other emotions or ideas.

Although not as wide in its appeal as the positive utopian qualities, distrust of England or, in its cruder forms, Anglophobia, was also a generally consistent feature of isolationism, probably its most distinctive feature. It, too, was essentially emotional rather than intellectual. Unlike the utopian elements of isolationism it was peculiarly American and stemmed from the ethnic mixture which was twentieth-century America.

Possibly ethnic and cultural affinity to land of origin is a deeply ingrained human trait, but it appears to diminish as new generations lose touch with the culture of their past. With diminishing resistance they accept and become a part of Anglo-American culture. For this reason, if for no other, ethnic isolationism and Anglophobia have weakened in the years since the First World War and particularly since the Second World War. They have no future. Conversely, ties with England have increased, particularly English dependence on American power, and the Anglo-American partnership has become less controversial.

The other elements of twentieth-century isolationism, except the always persistent appeal to tradition, were not consistent or deep-rooted. Since they were inconsistent and inharmonious they could not form the basis for a systematic ideology or theory of foreign relations. Even nationalism, a fairly constant ingredient, could not give isolationism the basis for a distinctive ideology. The anti-isolationists argued forcefully that they were better nationalists than were the isolationists and that their policies were more in the national interest. Isolationism as a whole was not a constant force nor a stable doctrine with a unique ideology. It fluctuated in response to given situations and reflected ideas and attitudes of the differing groups espousing it.

Lacking a firm ideology, isolationism cannot be explained primarily through the ideas of its leaders in specific situations. Composed of various emotional attachments, it at times took on the appearance of a cult. Intellectual consistency is not a criterion for the popularity of a doctrine. So it was with isolationism. Its greatest popular appeal was psychological and emotional.

Yet it cannot be explained exclusively in terms of emotional biases. It was an emotional and intellectual complex rooted in history. All Americans, regardless of ethnic origin, cultural bias, economic philosophy, or social attitude, could share the historical tradition of isolation, a utopia of the past. More than anything else twentieth-century isolationism was a tradition with a political following. At mid-century, however, the ideas of isolationism appeared incapable of stimulating a new, powerful political movement. "I have long insisted—and do now insist," said Dwight D. Eisenhower in November, 1952, before he won the Presidency, "that isolationism in America is dead as a political issue."

Five years later, in his second inaugural address, President Eisenhower said the mutual dependence of nations "makes isolation an impossibility. . . .No nation can longer be a fortress, lone and strong and safe. And any people, seeking such shelter for themselves, can now build only their own prison." But, like the endless hope for a lasting peace, the tradition and the utopian idea behind isolationism still live.

2. *Richard N. Current*

The United States and "Collective Security"

Notes on the History of an Idea

To reap the harvest of perpetual peace
By this one bloody trial of sharp war.
SHAKESPEARE, *King Richard III*

WHAT "collective security" has meant to Americans can be understood only after a review of the uses to which they have put the phrase or its equivalents from time to time. Essential to any definition, however, is the idea of co-operative action among the nations of the world to enforce peace. This idea must be distinguished from the concepts of world federation, neutrality, and power politics. World federation presupposes the merging of separate sovereignties into a super state, while collective security assumes the continuing sovereign independence of every nation great or small. It assumes, further, that in war time no nation rightfully can remain impartial as between a "peace-breaking" and a "peace-loving" party to the conflict, whereas neutrality in the traditional American sense connotes impartiality. Power politics refers to alliances directed toward a balance or a concert of powers, and, though these alliances may be designed ostensibly to keep the peace, they presumably are not the same as a combination in the interests of collective security. If upon examination they should prove to be the same—if collective security should signify no more than co-operative international action of whatever kind—then the phrase would appear to have little, if any, distinctive meaning.

I

Woodrow Wilson, honored as the founder of the League of Nations, believed that the League was essentially American

in its origin and nature.   Certainly the idea of enforcing peace—
a basic element of the League concept—had roots in American
experience, though not very deep ones.

Nineteenth-century Americans relied upon the progress of
moral principles and not upon economic or military power as a
means of eliminating war.   "Moral causes come into consideration in proportion as the progress of knowledge is advanced,"
Daniel Webster declared in 1824, expressing well the spirit of
his time, "and the public opinion of the civilized world is
rapidly gaining an ascendency over mere brutal force."   When,
in 1840, William Ladd, founder of the American Peace
Society, presented his plan for a world organization consisting
of a Congress of Nations and a Court of Nations, he counted
upon public opinion rather than physical power for enforcing
the decisions of the Court.

By the beginning of the twentieth century a few American
leaders were ready to espouse the idea of enforcing peace with
military power, at least in a limited or local way.   In 1898,
requesting authorization to use military and naval forces in
Cuba, President William McKinley called for the "forcible
intervention of the United States as a neutral to stop the war,
according to the large dictates of humanity" and also according
to "our aspirations as a Christian, peace-loving people."   In a
similar spirit, justifying intervention in Santo Domingo, President Theodore Roosevelt in 1904 said that the Monroe Doctrine, in cases of "chronic wrong-doing" in the Western Hemisphere, obliged the United States to exercise "an international
police power."   Six years later, addressing the Nobel Prize
Committee at Oslo, Roosevelt broadened the idea by suggesting the "establishment of some form of international police
power" which was to be exercised by "some combination between those great nations which sincerely desire peace."   But
he wished to exempt questions of "territorial integrity, honor,
and vital interest" from the jurisdiction of any international
tribunal to be set up.

With the outbreak of war in 1914, Roosevelt and many
others—in the Scandinavian countries, the Netherlands, and

Great Britain as well as the United States—offered a variety of peace-enforcement schemes. As early as August 6, 1914, the venerable former President of Harvard University, Charles W. Eliot, indignant at the invasion of Belgium, proposed to President Wilson "a combination of the British Empire, the United States, France, Japan, Italy, and Russia, in offensive and defensive alliance to rebuke and punish Austria-Hungary and Germany for the outrages they are now committing." This combination, Eliot said, would serve as "an effective international police method suitable to the present crimes" of the Central Powers. Replacing the outworn "balance of power," it would lead to "the future establishment and maintenance of federal relations and peace among the nations of Europe." Roosevelt, A. Lawrence Lowell, and William Howard Taft presented their peace-enforcement ideas in the homely and familiar American terms of the vigilance committee and the posse, as if international politics were comparable to the struggle between bad men and law-abiding citizens in the Wild West.

A number of more or less nebulous proposals were reduced to one and given a certain concreteness with the organization of the League to Enforce Peace and the formulation of its platform (June 17, 1915). This platform was notable for its narrowness—a fact often overlooked both at the time and afterward. It provided, first, for a "judicial tribunal" to hear only "justiciable questions"; second, for a "Council of Conciliation" to consider other questions; third, for the joint use by the "signatory Powers" of "both their economic and military forces against any one of their number that goes to war . . . *before any questions arising shall be submitted as provided in the foregoing*" (italics added); and fourth, for periodic conferences to "formulate and codify rules of international law." This platform included no guarantee of territorial integrity. In fact, the League to Enforce Peace was misnamed: it really stood (as a member of the much more thoroughgoing British League of Nations Society observed) for nothing more than a league to "enforce consideration," that is, to compel members to submit disputes to the judicial tribunal or the Council of Conciliation. Even so, the platform embodied too much force to suit old-fashioned pacifists such as William Jennings Bryan, the American Peace Society, and certain church groups. These people held fast to the nineteenth-century belief in the moral power of public opinion as the only appropriate sanction for peace.

Meanwhile President Wilson was groping toward his own vision of an organized and peaceful world. Ever since 1887, as a political scientist he had contemplated from time to time a rather vague notion of "governments joined with governments" throughout the world on a plan somehow similar to that of the federal union of American states. When war came to Europe in 1914, however, he reasserted the neutralist tradition and called for more than mere neutrality—for impartiality even in thought. Yet, privately, he referred to Eliot's proposal for an anti-German alliance as "momentous." While he refused to commit himself to any of the proposed peace plans, his thinking began early to diverge from that of the founders of the League to Enforce Peace. Before the end of 1914 (according to his brother-in-law Stockton Axson) he reached the following conclusion: "There must be an association of the nations, all bound together for the protection of the integrity of each, so that any one nation breaking from this bond will bring upon herself war; that is to say, punishment, automatically." He began to consider Colonel Edward M. House's suggestion of a Pan-American pact to "serve as a model for the European nations when peace is at last brought about"—a pact with "mutual guarantees of territorial integrity."

During 1915 and 1916 Wilson elaborated his association-of-the-nations idea in connection with his efforts to mediate and stop the fighting in Europe. Sir Edward Grey repeatedly urged upon the President a League of Nations as a means of eliminating "militarism and navalism" and assuring the "freedom of the seas." Doubtless Sir Edward had little more in mind than drawing the United States closer than ever to the Allies as the presumed foes of "militarism," but Wilson took seriously the idea of an early peace based upon an association of nations. Finding that both sides in the war avowed the same objective—"security"—he proposed to end the war with mutual guarantees of security reinforced by the power of the United States. "Our interest is only in peace and its guarantees," he told House (May 16, 1916); there must be "a universal alliance to maintain freedom of the seas and to prevent any war begun either a) contrary to treaty covenants or b) without warning and full inquiry,—a virtual guarantee of territorial integrity and political independence."

At this time Wilson did not contemplate American intervention on the side of the Allies. He thought such intervention would be unfortunate, for it might lead to the destruction of Germany and Austria-Hungary as powers, leaving Russia, Italy, and France more interested in dividing the spoils than in stabilizing the world. When, in 1916, under the auspices of the League to Enforce Peace, he publicly committed himself to an association of nations, critics attacked his scheme as looking toward an "entangling" alliance of the kind the Founding Fathers had warned against. With the universality of his league in mind, he replied that it was an alliance "disentangling" the peoples of the world from partial and conflicting combinations. Later (January 22, 1917) he explained that the new international arrangement must be based upon a compromise peace, a "peace without victory," since "only a peace between equals can last." There must be, he said, "not a balance of power, but a community of power." But Sir Edward Grey and the other Allied leaders put victory before peace. And the Germans, though expressing their willingness to join a league, soon announced their renewal of unrestricted submarine warfare.

When Wilson decided to lead the United States into the war, his idea of an association of the nations suffered a profound, though subtle, change. Recently he had been talking of an all-inclusive league, a "universal alliance," which was to be based on a "community" of power, not a balance and not predominance by any group of states. Now, in the war message (April 2, 1917), he spoke of what amounted to a *partial* league, a concert embracing only the "free peoples," the democratic nations, who alone could be trusted to "keep faith" and observe the "covenants." Whether he knew it or not, he now was advocating essentially what Eliot had recommended nearly three years before—a combination to punish Germany and then see to the future maintenance of peace. Apparently Wilson did have doubts about the consistency as well as the wisdom of his course. On the morning of the fateful April 2 he told Frank I. Cobb a war declaration "would mean that Germany would be beaten and so badly beaten that there would be a dictated peace, a victorious peace," according to Cobb's report. "The President said that such a basis was what the Allies thought they wanted, and that they would have their way in the very thing America had hoped against and struggled against." But Wilson overcame his doubts or at least submerged them in eloquence, reaffirming his foremost war aim thus (July 4, 1918): "that the world may be made safe for every peace-loving nation."

In the American debate over the League of Nations, partisan interest and personal spite had their place, and writers on the period have given adequate attention to them. Few writers have bothered to notice the real clash of ideas that occurred. The essential fact is that, before 1919, the league idea was still in flux and then, with the completion of the Covenant and the making of the world settlement, the idea became fixed and definite, its implications reasonably plain. What had been the question of *a* league was now the question of *the* League. Of those who had favored the one, not all had committed themselves wholeheartedly to the other.

The League to Enforce Peace had broadened its program by joining with the League of Free Nations Association in 1918 to support a combined "Victory Program." Yet, when accused of being a renegade from the league cause, Taft (in 1920) spoke truthfully in saying that the original platform of the League to Enforce Peace, which he had helped to sponsor, included no such plank as Article 10, by which the signatories of the Covenant agreed to respect one another's territorial and administrative integrity. Whatever may have been the motives of Henry Cabot Lodge in attaching reservations to the Covenant, or of Elihu Root in composing the "Statement of the Thirty-One," endorsing Warren G. Harding as the better "league" candidate in 1920, the reservationists without necessarily abandoning the notion of an international organization *of some kind* could and did point out that the Covenant of the Wilson League, with its Article 10, in effect pledged the United States "to go to war whenever war may be necessary" to sustain the integrity or independence of any member of the League. They concluded: "We cannot regard such a provision as necessary or useful for the league to preserve peace."

Many American critics of the League of Nations harked back to nineteenth-century views of the inappropriateness of physical power as a means of preventing war. "Senators," William E. Borah declared, "you cannot establish peace by force, by repression." And Robert Lansing, Wilson's Secretary of State, said: "I am willing to rely on the pacific spirit of democracies to accomplish the desirable relation between nations, and I do not believe that any League relying upon force or the menace of force can accomplish that purpose, at least for any length of time."

II

After the election of 1920 the issue of outright American membership in the League of Nations rapidly died, but the question of the relationship of the United States to the League remained alive. This question became a lively one indeed after the conclusion of the Kellogg Pact, or Pact of Paris, in 1928.

The origin of the Kellogg Pact was twofold. On the one hand, Aristide Briand sought an antiwar agreement with the United States as a means of supplementing his European treaty system and insuring security for France. On the other hand, American pacifists demanded that their country take a step toward the "renunciation" or the "outlawry" of war. Secretary of State Frank B. Kellogg was caught in a dilemma: if he rejected Briand's proposal, he would offend public opinion both abroad and at home; if he accepted it, he would commit his country to a foreign entanglement, to a kind of "negative military alliance." Finally Kellogg shifted the dilemma to Briand with a counterproposal that the antiwar agreement be enlarged so as to include all the nations of the world.

The upshot was the Pact of Paris, which bound the signatories to "renounce" war as an "instrument of national policy" and to seek solutions for their disputes "by pacific means." France and Great Britain signed with the explicit understanding that the treaty left them the full right to defend themselves as they saw fit. On behalf of the United States Kellogg himself announced the following official exegesis: "Every nation is free at all times and regardless of treaty provisions to defend its territory from attack or invasion and it alone is competent to decide whether circumstances require war in self-defense."

Looked upon in a matter-of-fact way, the Kellogg Pact might be considered as a minor diplomatic triumph for the American government—a successful device for avoiding an undesirable *démarche* without embarrassment. Viewed in a cynical light, it was "an international kiss." But American friends of the League saw the Pact with neither cynicism nor detachment. According to their reasoning, it revolutionized international law and the relation of the United States to the League.

David Hunter Miller, one of the drafters of the Covenant, asserted (1928) that "the treaty links the United States to the League as a guardian of the peace." Professor James T. Shotwell of Columbia University discovered (1929) in the preamble the "missing formula" which somehow associated the United States with the League. The preamble stated that any signatory seeking "to promote its national interests" by war "should be denied the benefits" of the Pact. From this it followed, according to Shotwell, that the United States as a signatory should co-operate at least passively in the application of League sanctions against another signatory whom the League had branded as an "aggressor." The United States might also co-operate actively, according to Professor Albert E. Hindmarsh of Harvard University. "Active co-operation of the United States in the work of preserving world peace by common action by no means presupposes that the United States must become a member of the League of Nations," Hindmarsh wrote (1933). "After all, through the Pact of Paris we are formally pledged to the principle upon which the Covenant is founded and which has constantly motivated every activity of the League since its creation."

Kellogg's successor in the State Department, Henry L. Stimson, guardedly endorsed the view of a revolutionized international law when (August 8, 1932) he declared that the Pact had begun a new era by making war "an illegal thing" and changing completely the old concept of neutrality. Most of the international lawyers in the United States, prominent among them Quincy Wright, accepted and elaborated the theory of the "new" international law. American publicists joined with their confreres from other countries at the Budapest Conference of the International Law Association in September, 1934, to agree upon an interpretation according to which the Pact exempted its signatories from old-fashioned neutral duties with respect to a fellow signatory who went to war in violation of it.

But the Pact provided no "machinery" of any kind for its own enforcement. Was it nevertheless meant to be enforced by the United States in co-operation with the League? The question could have been decided by the negotiation of supplementary treaties, and some of the believers in collective enforcement recommended that the United States undertake specific commitments by international agreement. But Shotwell himself doubted whether the Senate or the public would approve a treaty of that kind. "Indeed," he wrote (1936), "it was the absence of any formal provision for 'peace enforcement' which won to the support of the Pact that element of the American public who had opposed the Covenant of the League on account of Article 16" (the sanctions article). Advocates of peace enforcement therefore turned their attention to such partial measures as "consultation," "nonrecognition," and discriminatory arms embargoes.

The Hoover administration experimented from time to time with consultation, notably when, in 1931, an American officially sat with the League Council to consult regarding invocation of the Kellogg Pact against Japan. But President Hoover did not fully share his Secretary of State's conviction about the new dispensation in international law. He refused to let Stimson agree to a "consultative pact," though at the London Naval Conference of 1930 France refused to consent to any arms reduction unless the United States promised to "consult" with her in case her security was endangered. American champions of the scheme insisted that consultation was an innocent and neighborly act, utterly free from commitments for the use of armed force. Both of the major parties in 1932 approved consultation as a general principle ("consultation" in a general sense might mean any kind of diplomatic intercourse).

The Roosevelt administration authorized its representative at the Geneva disarmament conference to make (May 22, 1933) this pledge: "In the event that the states, in conference, determine that a state has been guilty of a breach of the peace in violation of its international obligations and take measures against the violator, then, if we concur in the judgment rendered as to the responsible and guilty party, we will refrain from any action tending to defeat such collective effort which these states may thus make to restore peace." This promise was not only well hedged about: it was also conditioned upon effective disarmament. This was as far as the United States in the 1930's went toward a commitment to consult, yet it was far enough to enable Cordell Hull afterward to assert: "Here, two and a half months after the new Administration came into power, was a radical change in the traditional attitude of this country toward two old principles—neutrality and freedom of the seas."

Nonrecognition was as ambiguous as consultation, or even more so. At the height of the Manchurian crisis Hoover recalled Bryan's nonrecognition policy of 1915, and Stimson proceeded to elaborate it as a corollary of the Kellogg Pact, informing Japan and China in identic notes (January 7, 1932) that the United States would not recognize territorial or other changes made in violation of American treaty rights. Where nonrecognition was to lead, Hoover and Stimson did not agree. The "Hoover-Stimson Doctrine" was really two doctrines, though its double meaning was not clear to the public at the time. In the Hoover Doctrine nonrecognition was the final step, and it was to be enforced only by the moral power of public opinion. In the Stimson Doctrine nonrecognition was a preliminary step, to be followed ultimately by economic and military sanctions imposed by the United States in co-operation with the League. At Stimson's urging, the League adopted the principle of nonrecognition, while censuring Japan, which forthwith resigned its League membership. Sanctions did not ensue, nor did legislation enabling the United States to reinforce sanctions.

As early as 1927, when the Kellogg Pact was still pending, a senator sponsored a resolution authorizing the President to prohibit the export of war materials to treaty violators, and in 1929 another senator proposed a similar embargo to apply against violators of the Pact. Both proposals were denounced as unneutral, and neither was passed. When the League was considering the Japanese question early in 1933, Senator Borah himself offered a more inclusive resolution to the effect that the President, after "securing the co-operation of such governments" as he deemed "necessary," might forbid the shipment of war materials "to such country or countries" as he might designate. President-Elect Roosevelt declared: "I have long been in favor of the use of embargoes on arms to . . . aggressor nations." Secretary Stimson sent a memorandum to inform the Senate that neutrality was a thing of the past; he hoped to discourage the senators from amending the Borah resolution so as to make it apply impartially against all nations at war. Despite the bipartisan support for a discriminatory embargo, no such measure became law.

Undaunted, the advocates of peace enforcement persisted in seeing a kind of magic in the Kellogg Pact. As late as 1934 a group of professors at the University of Chicago, including

Quincy Wright and Frederick L. Schuman, made the Pact the explicit basis for an ideal American foreign policy they undertook to design. By this time, however, the peace-enforcement people were about to acquire a new, more generalized formula. Hereafter, though they by no means forgot the Pact of Paris, they made fewer specific references to it. They now argued in terms of "collective security."

III

That phrase did not come into circulation in the United States until 1934, but it fast gained currency with the rise of Germany, Italy, and Japan as threats to the existing state of world affairs. In 1934 and again the following year the Committee on Collective Security of the League-sponsored International Studies Conference met in London, with American delegates present. The committee gave thought to several complex problems, including the problem of circumventing the apparent fear of the American people that they might become involved in a world war. "Neutrality, in their eyes, means essentially the possibility of remaining far from the field of battle," the committee's final report said. "Is it not then possible to devise for them a form of collaboration whose nature and characteristics would protect them against this risk?" This question indicated one of the committee's purposes. Professor C. A. W. Manning of the University of London suggested the purpose more pointedly when (August 22, 1935) he delivered before the Geneva Institute of International Relations a lecture on the new system of collective security. "The term 'Collective System' has not yet had either a long or a particularly stormy history," Manning remarked. "I suspect it was invented, quite recently, as a sly means of suggesting to the more 'soft-boiled' Americans that somehow their country, in signing the Kellogg Pact, had inadvertently and against its desires assumed a quasi-membership in the League."

As the term "collective security" acquired a somewhat longer and more stormy history, it also acquired a variety of conflicting connotations around its essential idea of enforcing peace.

Was the system to be all-inclusive? The report of the London committee said: "... if the notion of Collective Security does not require the organization of an absolutely worldwide system, it does assume the collaboration (in ways which may, however, be various) of a number of States which it is impossible to specify *ne varietur*, but which must be large enough to give it a quasi-universal character." Speaking at the University of Chicago in 1936, the English publicist Sir Alfred Zimmern defined the term as meaning "the safety of all by all." But Sir Alfred went on to say the "moral basis" for the system existed "only in the free, constitutional, and democratic states."

Did collective security depend on the League, and did it require that the League be reorganized? According to Zimmern, there was "no need for a new and more select League of Nations"; rather, "as between the free peoples, looser and more flexible arrangements" were "much to be preferred." But Edwin DeWitt Dickinson of Princeton University proposed a "universal league" for "consultation" only, with "regional undertakings" for sanctions within the various geographical areas of the world. "As regards the assurance of collective security," Dickinson said, "this probably means that we shall have a league of nations for Europe within the universal league." Writing that same year (1936) Shotwell defended the principle of "regionalism" and saw the League of Nations as developing from a "League to Enforce Peace" into a "League of Conferences" which the United States might well join as an "associate" rather than a fully committed member.

Was collective security a substitute for power politics? While the proponents of collective security said much of universality, and of regionalism within a universal system, they seldom argued in terms of the power balance and alliances, though Zimmern implied the formation of at least a loose alliance in proposing economic union and naval co-operation among the "free" states. Occasionally an advocate of collective security used the word *alliance* and made the explicit proposal that the United States actively manipulate the balance of power. Thus Denna Frank Fleming of Vanderbilt University urged (1938) that the United states assume its place at the center of the balance and declare its determination to stand by the League powers against Germany, Italy, and Japan. "Of course it will be said that to stand by the League now is merely to join one alliance," Fleming wrote. "So it would be." But it would be a "world alliance for peace."

Were "peace" and the *status quo* one and the same? Professor Philip C. Jessup of Columbia University stressed the point that the "stabilization of peace" could not be identified with the "stabilization of the *status quo*." James T. Shotwell said the "chief problem confronting international relations" was "the need for a more flexible structure than that which identifies justice with the *status quo*." Emphasizing the necessity for peaceful change, Dickinson wrote: "If security for the society of nations implies an assurance of orderly progress, collective security may be defined as co-operation in the attainment of such an assurance." But Fleming frankly stated that "some time a European *status quo* must be accepted as sufficiently definitive to be preferable to any continental war designed to end it" and that the "present map" was preferable to "wholesale slaughter" for establishing "perfect justice."

Would not the pursuit of collective security itself lead to wholesale slaughter, that is, to war? It most assuredly would not, according to Fleming, who based his reasoning on the supposition of an international law remade by the League Covenant and the Kellogg Pact. "It is true that in the last analysis the use of armies and navies on a major scale might result," Fleming conceded, "but such police measures, however large, would not be war. No collective action taken by a preponderance of the nations against an aggressor can hereafter be legally called war, nor be morally considered as war." Even Shotwell did not go so far as that. When the League makes provision for collective action, he explained, "it is not making provision for war any more than a State makes provision for murder when it sets up a police force." But Shotwell cautioned, "such a

conception of international solidarity would have to be recognized by nations outside the League as well as by those within it: it would be established only by a world-wide treaty."
And Quincy Wright observed (1940) that "coercive sanctions,
even if supported by the collective force of the community of
nations, if directed against a powerful state resemble war rather
than police."

While advocates of collective security thus differed among
themselves about its implications, opponents of the idea expressed no doubts as to its practical import.   In the United
States critics like Edwin M. Borchard and Charles A. Beard
maintained that if put into effect it would hinder peaceful
readjustments, hasten the day of general war, and involve this
country in the conflict.   In Great Britain E. H. Carr analyzed
the phrase as a device for confusing the real issues and protecting the "vested interest" of the satisfied powers.   "In the past,
Roman and British imperialism were commended to the world
in the guise of the *pax Romana* and the *pax Britannica*," Carr
wrote (1939).   "To-day, when no single Power is strong
enough to dominate the world, and supremacy is vested in a
group of nations, slogans like 'collective security' and 'resistance
to aggression' serve the same purpose of proclaiming an identity
of interest between the dominant group and the world as a
whole in the maintenance of peace."

In the United States the collective-security slogan appealed
to international-relations professors, to most of the peace societies, and to the Communist party, but not to the majority of
the people.   Opinion polls in 1935 indicated that comparatively
few Americans desired their government to act against "aggressors," or thought the world would be any worse off if the
League should be completely done away with.   Another poll
in 1937 revealed that more than 70 per cent believed it had
been a mistake to go to war in 1917.   This disillusionment with
the war to end war was reflected in the neutrality laws of 1935-
36-37, which authorized the President to embargo shipments
of arms to *both sides* in case he found a state of war existing.
The neutrality legislation became the focal issue as between

"internationalists" (those who favored collective security) and "isolationists" (those who opposed it). As in earlier years, the internationalists desired a discriminatory arms embargo. "Let us prevent war," they said. The isolationists supported the impartial principle of the law as it was. "Let us keep out of war," they said.

In this debate the Roosevelt administration took anything but a clear or consistent stand. Official statements appeared at times to share the internationalist view, at other times the isolationist, and most of the time a mixture of both. Secretary of State Cordell Hull spoke as a true isolationist when he said (September 15, 1936):

> I find as I review the line of foreign policy we have followed that we come close to Thomas Jefferson's expression—"peace, commerce, and honest friendship with all nations, entangling alliances with none."
>
> At times there has been criticism because we would not depart from our traditional policy and join with other governments in collective arrangements carrying the obligation of employing force, if necessary, in case disputes between other countries brought them into war. That responsibility, carrying direct participation in the political relations of the whole of the world outside, we cannot accept, eager as we are to support means for the prevention of war.

President Roosevelt sounded like an internationalist when, the next year, he came out with his suggestion that the "ninety per cent of the population of the world" who were "being jeopardized by the remaining ten per cent" should somehow set up a "quarantine" against the "contagion" of war, but what he meant by this he declined to say. When, in 1939, the President sought from Congress a repeal of the arms embargo, administration spokesmen referred to their substitute measure as another "neutrality" law, and they played upon both the isolationist keep-out-of-war theme and the internationalist prevent-war theme. "The basis for the recommendations made is the firm intention of keeping this country from being drawn into war," Secretary Hull assured all doubters, but at the same time he mentioned the government's efforts, "within the limitations of our traditional policy," to "do its utmost to avoid the outbreak of a general war."

After a general war nevertheless broke out, demonstrating that collective security was as yet an unrealized if not an unrealizable hope, the administration did not justify its policy of aiding the Allies on explicit grounds of collective security. On the whole the administration employed a simple theory of "self-defense," which seemed to be justified by the events of December 7, 1941. What followed was war, in Roosevelt's words a "war for survival," not a "police action."

IV

As the first World War had done, so too the second inspired in the United States a flurry of official and unofficial planning for the maintenance of the peace to come. And in both cases the resulting international organizations were essentially the same: the United Nations, though different in details, conformed in the main to the pattern of the defunct League. Yet the discussions of peace after 1941 differed in important respects from the discussion in earlier years. Most important, the ideas of military force and co-operative action became not only respectable but also popular. And when the Senate with little opposition voted for joining the UN, collective security at last seemed to prevail.

Unlike his predecessor during the First World War, President Roosevelt said little publicly about peace organization until the Second World War neared its close. What he did say indicated that he never gave thought, as Wilson briefly had done, to a truly universal plan and only belatedly gave much thought even to a "quasi-universal" one. Privately, Roosevelt by 1943 was thinking of a scheme by which the forces of Great Britain, Russia, China, and the United States would "police the world" after disarming the rest of the nations, including France. "He believed in the efficacy of direct personal contact between Churchill, Stalin, Chiang Kai-shek, and himself," Hull explained, "and he thought that this direct relationship among the chiefs of the four nations would result in efficient future management of the world." Beneath this partnership of power, Roosevelt found room for three separate "regional councils"—European, Oriental, and American— which were to have nothing to do with the enforcement of peace. He saw no need for a new world organization, a new League.

Meanwhile, both inside and outside the government, others got busy with more elaborate and more highly integrated plans. Immediately after the outbreak of the war the American Union for Concerted Peace Efforts, a combination of peace societies devoted to collective security, turned to the consideration of the "next peace." Soon Secretary Hull set up a semi-official Advisory Committee, to which he named Professor Shotwell, a key figure in the combined peace movement. "It is plain," Hull announced in a radio address (July 23, 1942), "that some international agency must be created which can—by force, if necessary—keep the peace among nations in the future." In 1943 the card-playing expert Eli Culbertson attracted a good deal of attention with his plan for a "World Police Force" in which a permanent "mobile corps," recruited from the smaller states, would outnumber the separate "national contingents" to be provided in emergencies by the big powers. Finally President Roosevelt gave public endorsement to the idea of a general organization with force at its command when (June 15, 1944) he issued a statement which Hull, with the Advisory Committee, had prepared. "The maintenance of peace and security must be the joint task of all the peace-loving nations," the statement read. "We are seeking effective agreement and arrangements through which the nations would maintain, according to their capacities, adequate forces to meet the needs of preventing war."

Almost unanimously the wartime peace planners emphasized force—armed force. Almost alone, former President Herbert Hoover dissented. In a book he wrote with Hugh Gibson (published in 1942; reprinted as a Book-of-the-Month-Club offering in 1943) Hoover argued that military or economic force could not bring lasting peace either through alliances or through a League of Nations. "After all," he wrote, "the preservation and advancement of civilization cannot be based on force." Only through the advancement of civilization, and only by "pacific methods," could the world attain permanent peace.

Hoover was echoing a tradition that was old in American thinking, at least as old as Daniel Webster and William Ladd, but by the time Hoover's book appeared, that tradition already was a casualty of war. Opinion polls in 1942 and 1943 indicated that the American people, or most of them, no longer put their trust in the progress of moral principles. By the end of 1943 three-fourths of the people questioned were ready for the United States to join an international organization and support an "international police force." Few of the people paid much attention to the "world plans" then under discussion in radio programs, newspapers, and books. But, as an opinion analyst commented, "The police force doctrine . . . is simple. So familiar is it that people need hardly understand in order to approve." The "police symbol" appealed to them. "It is active, American."

While the UN Charter was emerging from the Dumbarton Oaks and San Francisco conferences, the police symbol figured prominently in the campaign, both official and unofficial, to educate the public for approval of the UN. "The council of the United Nations must have the power to act quickly and decisively to keep the peace by force if necessary," Roosevelt said in a speech (October 21, 1944) advocating the Dumbarton Oaks proposals. "A policeman would not be a very effective policeman if, when he saw a felon break into a house, he had to go to the Town Hall and call a town meeting to issue a warrant before the felon could be arrested." With Theodore Roosevelt, international politics had been reducible to the analogy of the posse or the vigilance committee. With Franklin D. Roosevelt, it was the village constable.

When the final Charter appeared, its most distinctive feature was the provision for armed forces to be made available to the Council for instant use. Without this provision (which never went into effect) the Charter looked like little more than a redraft of the League Covenant. Yet Americans expected much of the UN plan. "We must have collective security to stop the next war, if possible, before it starts," said Senator Arthur H. Vandenberg in announcing his bipartisan support of UN membership, and there were few to disagree with him. Once the Senate had given its nearly unanimous approval, believers in collective security rejoiced. They had convinced themselves that the Second World War came in consequence of a "great betrayal"—the refusal of the United States to live up to Wilson's ideals and join the League. By this reasoning it followed that a third world war should never come, for this time the United States was fulfilling its obligation, was joining the UN.

Amid the general optimism, only a small minority of Americans raised any doubts. Most of the doubters belonged to either of two groups, the one idealistic, the other realistic. Writing (1945) as an idealistic champion of true world government, Emery Reves denounced Roosevelt's policeman analogy as fallacious and the idea of basing peace on big-power unanimity as worthy of Alice in Wonderland and as indicative of either the "naïveté" or the "monstrous hypocrisy" of government leaders. "Collective security without collective sovereignty is meaningless," Reves contended. Speaking from a realistic point of view, Frederick L. Schuman both agreed and disagreed with Reves. "Politics under anarchy is power politics, since no other kind of politics is possible without world government," Schuman said (July, 1945). "And since nothing deserving to be called world government is on the horizon, the problem of peace remains a problem of power politics." Quite fanciful was the concept of an association of fifty-odd sovereignties "all pledged to keep the peace through the coercion of the peace-breaking sovereignties by the collective power of the peace-loving sovereignties," though that concept was the essence of contemporary international law. "For an indefinite future, Washington, Moscow, and London either will rule the world together or will ruin the world in a new rivalry among themselves for global hegemony."

Within a few weeks after Schuman spoke, the explosions over Hiroshima and Nagasaki gave a grim literalness to his words: "ruin the world." When the struggle for hegemony—the "cold war"—came to light, the prospect grew even more grim. And when the Russians began to share the secrets of atomic fission and fusion, the idea of collective security ran against facts more ineluctable than ever. "Atomic and bacteriological weapons have made nonsense of any agreement by separate nations to act together to protect a nation that has been attacked," wrote (1948) Cord Meyer, Jr., a veteran who had lost an eye in the Second World War and then had attended the San Francisco UN conference. "If the Security Council did order military forces into action against a small nation," Meyer added, after noting that the Council was estopped from sending such forces against a big power, "it would be hypocrisy to call this 'police action.'" ". . . Violence can be justified as police action only when it is employed to enforce an established law that applies equally to all."

When President Harry S. Truman sent armed forces to South Korea in 1950, he nevertheless described this as a police action and a venture in collective security. Meanwhile, as the Truman administration set to fashioning an elaborate system of alliances, its spokesmen justified this policy by citing the Charter's provisions regarding "regional" and "self-defense" arrangements, even though the arrangements in the making obviously were directed against a fellow UN member. According to Secretary of State Dean Acheson there was no contradiction between regional and universal security: the one contributed to the strengthening of the other. In a speech to the General Assembly of the UN (September 20, 1950) Acheson said:

I have already stressed the importance we attach to the United Nations as the framework of an effective system of collective security. The steps we take to strengthen our collective security are not only essential to the survival of the United Nations but will contribute positively toward its development. The close ties of a common defense are developing an added cohesion among regional groups. This is a significant step toward a closer relationship among nations. . . .

The United States also attaches importance to the universal character of the United Nations, which enables it to serve as a point of contact between the Soviet Union and the rest of the world during the period of tension.

The Eisenhower administration continued the pact-making process and continued to argue its constitutionality in terms of the Charter, using the phrase "collective security" as a synonym for the system of alliances.

Certain political scientists and men of affairs clearly saw and frankly stated the practical value which the UN and the idea of collective security had for the United States. "In the struggle against Soviet imperialism, it is vital that we have firm friends and willing allies who recognize mutual interests. We can best assure their co-operation by preserving and strengthening the tenuous ties by which all are bound together within the United Nations." So wrote Kenneth W. Thompson, then (1953) of Northwestern University. "Perhaps the supreme paradox of American foreign policy today is the necessity placed upon us to seize and employ the essentially utopian instruments of collective security in a brutally realistic power struggle." Apparently sharing this view was a discussion group of experts, including Chester Bowles and W. Averell Harriman, who met from 1953 to 1955 at the Council on Foreign Relations in New York, and whose discussions provided the basis for a book (1956) written by Henry L. Roberts of the Russian Institute, Columbia University. Noting the possibility of finding in the UN ideal "a broadly accepted *authority* or *legitimacy*" for the American system of alliances, Roberts explained that he did not mean "substituting the UN for the alliances." "We mean rather that only by the act of supporting and working for the objectives of the UN Charter can we make them meaningful to the interests of the nations, and that only in an international atmosphere where these objectives remain alive and relevant can a democratic alliance have much chance of finding a broader sense of purpose and cohesiveness than one of bare expediency." Bare expediency, that is to say, was not expedient for the United States.

Times indeed had changed. Once, in the 1930's, it had seemed advisable for policy makers, regardless of their policy, to express themselves in the language of isolationism and neutrality. In the 1950's it seemed advisable to speak in terms of collective security.

In the history of this idea, however, the real turning point had come much earlier. It was in 1917. Until February of that year President Wilson had advanced toward a concept truly ecumenical in its essence and highly promising in its implications—the concept of an association of *all* the nations which was to be based upon a compromise to end the war with a "community" of power and without victors or vanquished. Wilson abandoned the distinctive elements of that idea when the final clash came between his interpretation of the freedom of the seas and the German use of the submarine. Thereafter, for the next forty years, whatever the phrase or the fervor with which it was expressed, the idea of collective security never amounted to much more than a new vehicle for old baggage. True, the League and the UN were more highly organized and more broadly inclusive in membership than old-fashioned alliances (and, incidentally, they performed valuable non-political functions which those alliances did not). True also, the systems of collective security were designed for "police action" against an "aggressor," not for "war" against an "enemy." In these respects collective security was, perhaps, new. In fundamentals it was hard to distinguish from the timeworn statecraft of alliances designed to achieve for their adherents some kind of "balance," which usually meant predominance.

3. J. Chalmers Vinson

Military Force and American Policy, 1919-1939

Justice without force is impotent. Force without Justice is tyrannical. We must therefore combine Justice with force.

PASCAL

FREDERICK THE GREAT once observed that "diplomacy without armaments is like music without instruments." There is ample evidence that Europeans accepted Frederick's dictum. American statesmen of the nineteenth century, however, often denied the theory that military force was an inseparable and legitimate part of foreign policy and denounced the European concept of *Realpolitik*. Early in the century they stated the principle that the sole purpose of military establishments was defense. Diplomacy should be backed by legal and moral sanctions only. In nineteenth-century America, largely isolated from disputes of the European continent, such a passive policy was practical as well as idealistic and served the nation's needs in defense and diplomacy. The nonmilitary approach to diplomacy gradually became a tradition.

With the twentieth century and a changed world, America grew more vulnerable to military attack and more involved in world politics. The logic of a diplomacy divorced from military force became less clear. Indeed, during the First and Second World Wars a nonmilitary policy was rejected in theory and in practice. During the long armistice between these conflicts, however, the traditional separation of diplomat and soldier was reaffirmed. For good or ill, American foreign policy returned to the traditional reliance on moral force and public opinion. Defense became the sole duty of the small military forces maintained during the interwar years.

The American nation heeded well the advice of Thomas

Jefferson to preserve its republican ideals by guarding "the supremacy of the civil over the military authority." There seemed to be little disagreement with Woodrow Wilson's warning at the close of the First World War: "You know how impossible it is, in short, to have a free nation, if it is a military nation and under military order." The Prussian ideal as expressed in the maxim that war was a continuation of diplomacy by other means could not flourish in the America of 1919-1939.

Far from co-ordinating force and diplomacy, the American statesmen and people set the two up as incompatible. Diplomacy should be employed to abolish war. Peace was established as the goal of American foreign policy. Rejection of the League of Nations established legal and moral force rather than military force as instruments for achieving peace. Such were the ideals reiterated by America's leaders during the interwar period. Charles Evans Hughes, as Secretary of State, described his agency as the Department of Peace. The laconic Calvin Coolidge, during his presidency, reduced all of American foreign policy to the one word, peace. His Secretary of State, Frank B. Kellogg, helped negotiate in August of 1928 a treaty renouncing war as an instrument of national policy. A few weeks later, President Herbert Hoover asserted: "The European nations have by the Covenant of the League of Nations, agreed that if nations fail to settle their differences peaceably, then force should be applied by other nations to compel them to be reasonable. We have refused to travel this road. We are confident that at least in the Western Hemisphere public opinion will suffice to check violence."

Whereas the Harding and Coolidge administrations spoke of the preservation of peace in ideal terms, the Hoover administration was faced soon with the actual outbreak of war between China and Japan. Should force be used to preserve peace? "The United States has never set out to preserve peace among other nations by force," was Hoover's answer. Cordell Hull, speaking for the Roosevelt administration, rejected many times the theory of force as an instrument of diplomacy. "All nations should," he said in March of 1938, "through voluntary self-restraint, abstain from use of force in pursuit of policy and from interference in the internal affairs of other nations." Further evidence of the Roosevelt administration's policy was its rejection of a request for long-range bombers by the Army Air Force in 1938 on the ground that "our national policy contemplates preparation for defense, not aggression."

All these pronouncements on policy of the 1920's and 1930's, these statements in favor of maintaining peace by persuasion and example rather than force, found enthusiastic endorsement by the American public. The traditional distrust of strong military establishments and the desire for peace were increased by the public's universal demand for lower taxes. Defining the public mind is a difficult task, but in the matter of using military force for purposes of foreign policy, opinion during the interwar period was clear. The public demanded small military establishments. Military force as an instrument of foreign policy was rejected at the Washington Conference, in the Kellogg-Briand Pact, and in the neutrality legislation of the 1930's. In each instance public approval in the United States reached an almost religious fervor. The few voices that called for co-ordination of military and diplomatic policy could not be heard.

I

Co-ordination of military and diplomatic policy was rendered impossible from the outset of the postwar era by the return to the idea of armed forces too small for any but defensive purposes.

A trend toward naval supremacy, initiated by Theodore Roosevelt, made little headway under his immediate successors. It was picked up again in 1916 when Congress, under the threat of war, passed an act to provide a navy second to none. Enthusiasm for such a program faded at the end of the war with the program far from completion. Wilson sought to take advantage of the antimilitaristic mood to promote the

League of Nations. Membership in the League was the only alternative to naval supremacy, he argued. The Senate, in 1919-1920, rejected the League but did not want naval supremacy. At the Washington Conference the Five-Power Treaty provided for the limitation of armament on a basis of parity with Great Britain. The cost of armament was reduced while the relative naval strength of the United States remained unchanged.

Actually the 5-5-3 ratio of the Five-Power Treaty was not maintained by the United States during the next decade. Less than half the tonnage allowed by treaty was built. Even so, it was difficult to get the personnel to man the ships. Not until 1933 was a program undertaken to reach Washington Conference treaty strength; not until 1936 were steps taken to meet the challenge of the Japanese navy. Large appropriations were made in the following years, but American naval experts testified, shortly before the outbreak of World War II, that the Navy had only one-third the force needed to take the offensive in the Far East.

As for the Army during the 1920's and 1930's, it was almost abolished. Congress in 1920 passed a National Defense Act authorizing an army of not more than 280,000 enlisted men, but appropriations for the Army were so small that it did not reach the maximum figure until 1940. The Army stood at 150,000 in the year 1921, and reached its lowest ebb in 1933 at 122,000. More important was the fact that the authorized force of 280,000 was to have been a minimum as well as a maximum, based on the concept of skeletal units that could quickly expand. When this theory was disregarded and the enlistments dropped below the recommended figure, efficiency as well as size was reduced. Further checks on the Army were sought in 1922 by members of the House of Representatives who recommended withholding pay for troops in excess of definite geographical quotas established by Congress. Under this plan there were to be no soldiers in China, not more than 500 in Europe, 5,000 in Panama, and 5,000 in the Hawaiian

Islands. The measure met defeat, but the theory behind it made a marked impression on officials of the State Department.

Opposition of Congress and the public to building strong military forces frequently demonstrated itself, of course, in the general management of foreign affairs. At the Washington Conference antimilitarism was the touchstone of policy. Secretary Hughes attempted to reconcile an active foreign policy with a minimal military force. Thus he agreed to maintain the *status quo* on Pacific island fortifications although the General Board of the Navy advised against any discussion of the islands, and utterly opposed any restriction on fortification. His policy was based on the assurance by his senatorial colleagues on the delegation that no appropriation for fortifications could be carried through anyway.

After the Conference of 1921-1922, Hughes reflected in his policy toward China his consciousness of the limitations placed upon him—the lack of military force behind his diplomacy. The United States, he concluded, would never go to war over any aggression on the part of Japan in China. He reiterated this in 1922 with the statement that it was "no part of his Government's purpose to impress upon the Chinese Government or people the military power or prestige of this country." Two years later he explained again the impossibility of controlling the situation in China by a display of force. Congress, he said, had not provided the necessary troops, and public opinion in this country would not sanction the dispatch of additional military forces to China "unless in the event of some impending castatrophe such as the Boxer Movement."

Hughes could not apply his ideas on policy in a peaceful era, but his successors, President Hoover and Secretary of State Henry L. Stimson, faced an "impending catastrophe" when Japan moved into Manchuria in 1931. In agreement with the ban on military force, Hoover and Stimson sought to check the challenge of Japan by diplomatic means: a policy of nonrecognition. As to the meaning of this policy, they could not agree. Nonrecognition was an end itself for Hoover; there would be no sanctions. Military strength, Hoover believed, should be limited to the sole purpose of national defense; it should not be employed as the agent of peace; progress in promoting peace could come only in the "moral field as distinguished from the force field." Stimson occasionally suggested economic sanctions as a supplement to nonrecognition, but Hoover looked upon these as a form of force which would lead to war. The President remained firm in his determination to rely solely on "diplomatic pressure and the power of world public opinion." He later recalled that Stimson was "at times more of a warrior than a diplomat." Stimson's form of nonrecognition backed by economic sanctions won verbal approval by the Roosevelt administration, but no action resulted. Even when the League of Nations officially adopted nonrecognition in March, 1932, nothing occurred to change the course of international affairs.

Secretary of State Hull, taking over for Stimson in 1933, continued for a time the Hughes-Hoover-Stimson policy of attempting to "stay Japan's hand" by measures short of war or any show of military force. When in 1934 he reached the "Oriental crossroads of decision," he determined to maintain the Open Door policy. This, he recalled in his memoirs, required a firm, though not aggressive, policy toward Japan. Hull added that "it meant adequate military preparedness." Such a policy was strongly advocated by Ambassador Joseph C. Grew, in Tokyo during the 1930's. He recommended to the State Department a Navy of treaty strength and the maintenance of 5:3 ratio over Japan "regardless of cost should Japan exceed the treaty limits." But the adequate military preparedness on which Hull sought to rest his policy was not available even during the crucial negotiations of the latter 1930's.

From 1898 to 1934 the United States did employ in the Caribbean area, in contrast to other areas, a policy based on military force. Military measures in central and South America clearly promoted the security of the United States. This fact was recognized in the nineteenth century when American policy sought to prevent strong powers from gaining a foothold in or near the Caribbean. With construction of the Panama

Canal, the Caribbean became a vital area in national defense.
The general policy of avoiding the use of force did not apply.
No one doubted the right of self-defense. Furthermore professional military forces, not citizen armies, carried out the
necessary interventions in the Caribbean. Even these circumstances did not make the policy of intervention popular with
the American public. Senators of the Progressive wing, demanding that a line be drawn between national defense and
economic imperialism, constantly attacked intervention in the
Caribbean.

Still, the traditional military-diplomatic policy of the
United States in the Caribbean—like American policy toward
the rest of the world—could not withstand the pacifism of the
postwar era. Wilson in his first administration denounced
armed intervention in principle but frequently found it necessary in fact. In the 1920 presidential campaign, Senator Warren G. Harding attacked Wilson's policy of military intervention. Hughes, in 1923, went so far as to deny that any right
of overlordship could be derived from the Monroe Doctrine.

The idea of intervention, as incorporated in the Roosevelt Corollary of 1905, received a mortal blow with the publication in 1930 of the Clark Memorandum on the Monroe Doctrine. Franklin D. Roosevelt, in 1933, went further with the
declaration that the "definite policy of the United States from
now on is opposed to armed intervention." This development was climaxed in 1938 by the Declaration of Lima—the
peace and security and territorial integrity of all the American republics was the common concern of all.

With the continentalizing of the Monroe Doctrine the
United States renounced military force as the basis of its relations with other countries in the Western Hemisphere and
especially in the Caribbean, the area of the world most vital
to American peace and security. Isolation from Europe had
always been far more complete than isolation from the Far
East or the Caribbean. Military force did not receive serious
consideration as an agent of American policy in that area during the long armistice.

II

Military force as an agent of foreign policy had long been decried by the peace movement in the United States. From the early nineteenth century, zealot advocates of peace worked ardently against the use of force, favoring instead some form of international organization as the surest means to establishing a peaceful world order. Enforcement of decisions by such a supernational body would, in the various plans advanced by American peace enthusiasts, be carried out by the moral force of public opinion. An early champion of peace, William Ladd, author, in 1840, of a constitution for a congress of nations, believed public opinion was a force more righteous than military power and ten times as strong.

A shift from faith in moral sanctions took place at about the opening of the twentieth century. Representative Richard Bartholdt, a devoted worker for peace, in 1904 brought before Congress a resolution for compulsory arbitration. This plan failed, but six years later Bartholdt was largely responsible for adoption by the House of Representatives of a similar resolution. It provided that the President should set up a five-man commission to consider the possibility of using existing international agencies to limit armament and combine "the navies of the world into an international force for the preservation of universal peace." President Taft did not act on this resolution. Congress, undaunted, passed a resolution for disarmament in 1913. Unlike the measure of 1910, this resolution provided for no international military force to be placed at the disposal of the proposed world organization. This renunciation of force represented a new trend in congressional thinking on world organization. It was interrupted briefly but ineffectively by a number of resolutions for international police action in 1915, just after the First World War had broken out in Europe. But Congress voted down a specific proposal to establish an international police force when it wrote an amendment calling for disarmament into the Naval Appropriations Bill of 1916. The Borah Resolution of 1920, which to a degree was responsible for the Washington Conference for naval disarmament, contained no hint of a world peace organization, a feature of all earlier congressional plans for disarmament, or of any use of military force to maintain international order.

Apart from Congress, many important leaders in America worked for peace in the first two decades of the century. Only two of these, Andrew Carnegie and Theodore Roosevelt, placed any emphasis on military sanctions as a means to guarantee peace. The beginning of war in Europe changed this thinking, as it had done before and would do again. Military force became an important part of the plans of the League to Enforce Peace by the time it was formally organized in 1915. Under this plan joint military action would compel nations to seek arbitration or conciliation of disputes before undertaking hostilities. Woodrow Wilson, who had proposed joint guarantees of territorial and political integrity in the Pan American Treaty of 1915, incorporated the theory of force for peace in Article 10 of the Covenant of the League of Nations.

This move was, however, contrary to sentiment in Congress, and there was no general unanimity of opinion in the United States favoring this trend toward military sanctions. William Jennings Bryan and Elihu Root were able representatives of the opposition to such leaders as Carnegie and Roosevelt. Another opponent of force in foreign policy was Robert Lansing, one of Wilson's advisers, who did not believe that so important a break with tradition as Article 10 of the League Covenant would receive support from the American people or approval from the Senate. The President, in defense of Article 10, denied the break with the tradition of nonentanglement. There was "no entangling alliance in a concert of power," he asserted. In the covenant nations united "to act in the same sense and with the same purpose." It was absolutely essential to assume an obligation to use force, to break with old practice. Yet this would not cause the United States to embark on a long series of wars, for force would be the last resort rather than the first. Arbitration and economic boycott would serve as a substitute for war, and in actual practice there would "be no need for force." It was the first sentence in Article 10 providing for mutual respect of territorial integrity, said Wilson, that was "the solemn thing," rather than the second sentence providing for consultation. The Covenant was a "constitution of peace, not a league of war," declared Wilson as he sought to convince his fellow citizens that the world organization would probably never use force. At the same time, the nation must stand ready to honor its pledge should the highly unlikely situation demanding action develop.

In retrospect, it is clear that elimination of Article 10, as demanded by both foes and friends of the treaty, was in accord with the general feelings of the American people after the First World War. As the Senate debate demonstrated, a major objection to the Article was its solemn moral obligation to act. If this pledge were honored, American diplomacy would sacrifice its cardinal quality, independence of action. American policy would be subject to the whims and dictates of "foreign gentlemen at Geneva." Injustice would result, so many Senators argued, from the terms of the Treaty of Versailles—an attempt of victors to divide the spoils and freeze the *status quo* as of the date of division. The real purpose of the League—and, in particular, Article 10—was not to establish a just peace but to enlist the military power of the United States in "nailing down" the unjust *status quo*. The nonmilitary traditions of the United States were cited and fear that use of military force would undermine American democracy was aroused. Other senators asserted that the cost of continual resort to military force would bankrupt the United States without substantially aiding the cause of world peace.

An important elder statesman, Elihu Root, added his warnings against Article 10 to those of the Senate. He had never favored coercion by military force as a factor in world peace, and had refused to join the League to Enforce Peace. Although he did write Wilson in 1918 that a breach of the peace should concern every member of the community of nations, it was not long before Root concluded that in the world of 1919 there was no community of nations. Americans would reject any outside "control over national independence of action,"

and refuse to honor the pledges on which an effective organization could arise.   Lord Bryce wrote Root at this time that the
same condition existed in England.   It was futile to draft an
Article 10, Bryce said, because Englishmen would never act
unless the national interest of England was clearly in jeopardy.

In addition to his public statements on the treaty, Root
spent much time in advising Lodge and other senators on
treaty reservations.   After much conferring and negotiating,
the Senate adopted a long and involved reservation to Article
10: the United States government accepted no obligation to
preserve the political and territorial integrity of other nations,
and would take no action in such cases except as Congress
deemed necessary and approved by joint resolution.

Root, who wished to eliminate it, and Wilson, who felt
it to be foundation of the League, thought this reservation was
a crippling blow, a nullification of Article 10.   When the anal-
ogous terms of such present-day agreements as the North Atlantic Treaty and the United Nations Charter are recalled, this
reservation does not appear so extreme.   The point is, however, that in 1920 it did not seem likely that Congress would
authorize military action.   Certainly there is little evidence
in the history of the next two decades to refute the view.

In retrospect it is clear that America's final rejection of military force to preserve peace and final rejection of the League of
Nations came with the campaign of 1920.   The drift of Harding's conflicting statements was that the United States should
reject the League.   In its place should rise a "society of free
nations or an association of free nations or a league of free
nations."   This stand was by no means clear to all in 1920,
but it was sufficiently apparent to anger many pro-League
Republicans and goad them to action.   They issued a statement—the Appeal of the Thirty-one—drafted by the ubiq-
uitous Elihu Root, advocating that America work with other
nations to amend the existing Covenant.   When an effective
league had developed, the United States should join it.   The
Democrats had rejected any modification of the League and
any compromise; consequently the Republican party alone

could carry the nation into a practical league for peace. The Appeal agreed with Harding's characterization of the League as an "offensive and defensive alliance of great powers" in conflict with the American ideal of a "society of free nations." The former system stood on military might and self-interest, the latter on respect for law and justice. The Thirty-one, who professed to favor the League, agreed that one of the major defects was insistence on military sanctions; the United States should drop Article 10 entirely.

Root insisted privately that the Republican position on the League issue not be one of adamant opposition, as Borah and Hiram Johnson had wished, or the plan of the Republican National Chairman Will Hays—declaring the League dead and "erecting on the foundation of The Hague an enduring peace built on law and justice rather than diplomacy and force." The real issue, according to Root, should be the Wilson League based on force versus an "Americanized" League based on law. Failure to advocate a league of some sort, he knew, would result in loss of support of clergymen, women, and other good Republicans.

Harding had won the election of 1920 with the vague promise of some sort of an association of nations. Secretary of State Charles E. Hughes quickly reached the conclusion in 1921 that Harding would not support any movement toward the League. As a member of the cabinet, Hughes explained that he felt it necessary to support the President and accede to the demands of the Senate irreconcilables that there be no league or association. Although Hughes had signed the Appeal of the Thirty-one and considered working for adoption of the League, he concluded that a fight would gain nothing while forfeiting all hope for a harmonious administration. Furthermore, Hughes had little personal enthusiasm for a League of Nations backed by force, and popular demand for such a league had cooled with the end of the war.

In the United States after 1921 there was indeed a great, an apparently almost universal, revulsion against war or armament or military coercion to enforce peace. A plan for peace

typical of this mood was presented by Senator Porter Mc-
Cumber, once an advocate of the League and of Article 10.
McCumber called for an association of nations, but he stipulated
that it not be backed by force or threat of force. Rather it
was to rest "entirely upon the sacred national honor of each
Government, supported by an informed public conscience
that will not brook any international injustice." Senator Mc-
Cumber's conversion from Article 10 to more pacific methods
signified a trend. Senator Borah's position demonstrated no
trend; but in a speech, September, 1921, he clearly expressed an
opinion which the majority of the Senate had reached. "One
of the revolting monstrosities born of the war, the legitimate
offspring of secret diplomacy and violence, is the absurd,
iniquitous belief that you can only have peace through martial
means—that force, is the only power on earth with which to
govern men. I denounce the hideous, diabolical idea, and I
insist that this Government ought to be counted against all
plans, all treaties, all programs, all policies based on this
demoniacal belief." Again he declared that there had been
two thousand years of the worship of force. He asked:
"What are the fruits? If anyone is familiar with the vernacular
of Hell, let him undertake to paint the picture. Human
tongue is inadequate to the task."

From this assumption Borah and others advanced a sort of
doctrine of the two hemispheres in relation to the use of force.
In the Old World the essence of all plans for preserving peace
had been employment of military sanctions—creation in a
new form of the old system of alliances. In the New World
the American system for peace stood on the acceptance of moral
sanctions, trusting in the conscience of nations to make it opera-
tive.

Secretary Hughes at the Washington Conference of 1921-
1922 sought to translate rejection of force by the American
people into sound foreign policy. He hoped that the resurgence of China would be fostered by the Nine-Power Treaty
and that peaceful checks on Japan's ambitions to expand, in the
Four-Power Pact, would stabilize the Far East. Moral sanc-

tions without any recourse to military force formed the foundations of these treaties.

During the debates on the Washington Conference treaties a determination to abjure force was most evident in the arguments advanced in the Senate. Such men as James Reed, Johnson, and Borah saw in Article 2 of the Four-Power Treaty, which provided for consultation to follow a failure to settle differences through diplomatic channels, the same legal and moral obligations to use force provided by Article 10 of the League Covenant. Hughes and Harding, however, had sought to anticipate this opposition and free the treaty of any obligation. Harding, in presenting the treaties to the Senate, asserted: "The conclusions reached and the covenants written neither require nor contemplate compulsive measures against any power in the world, signatory or nonsignatory. The offerings are free will; the conscience is that of world-opinion; the observance is a matter of national honor . . . . There are mutual and essential interests affecting the welfare and peace of all nations, and they cannot be promoted by force." Lest some obtuse Senator fail to get his message, Harding specified that the treaty contained "no commitment to armed force, no alliance, no written or moral obligation to join in defense, no expressed or implied commitment to arrive at any agreement except in accordance with a constitutional method." Thus he eliminated military sanctions and the force of the treaty derived from "moral warnings" and the "focus of world opinion on a given controversy."

The Senate, skeptical of this and later administration assurances that force would not be used, incorporated this pledge given by Harding in the Brandegee Reservation to the Four-Power Treaty. The largest vote given any of the Washington Conference treaties or any of the many proposed reservations to treaties in the Senate was the 93 to 0 vote for the Brandegee Reservation. Had the balloting been close, this reservation might have been dismissed as no more than an effort to obstruct the treaty. But no senator opposed the reservation.

During the debate even those defending the Four-Power

Treaty in the Senate disavowed collective military force, refusing to undertake obligations or make commitments. They devoted much time to explaining that there was little possibility that the treaty would be invoked, for it related to an area where trouble was unlikely to develop. But even if the impossible occurred and conflict developed, the treaty provided for consultation, not action.

Although Secretary of State Hughes reflected congressional and popular opinion in his pronouncements, his policy derived from his own convictions as well as from political expediency and the power of Congress. The theory of military force as an aid to peace he denounced. As befitted his legal background, he favored "the reign of law, as distinguished from the rule of might"; he believed that the way to peace was through agreement, not through force. The effort to promote law "as accepted, not imposed, may be after all the most important contribution to permanent peace." Force in itself could never be an effective instrument of peace, for, when nations exhausted peaceful means of settlement, they would be moved in their use of power "not by principle but by national expediency." Hence, the use of force degenerated inevitably into the unholy politics of balance-of-power. Only when there was a will for peace could there be force for peace. Great powers, when they disagreed, could allow no restraint and would resort to war. "All contrivances for maintaining peace by economic pressure, as well as by military force, fail when the test comes. There is no path to peace except as the will of peoples may open it." Hughes felt that his country was still opposed, "as it had been in Monroe's time," to alliances, and also to commitments in advance "with respect to the employment of the power of the United States in unknown contingencies." The policy of the nation for the next century, Hughes believed, should be the policy of the Harding administration: independence and co-operation. "Independence—that does not mean and never has meant isolation. Co-operation—that does not mean and never has meant alliances or political entanglements."

In developing co-operation for world peace, the League

of Nations was a constant problem. Harding in 1920 had pronounced the organization "deceased." It continued to live. The very existence of the League was a living reproach and challenge to its enemies, who were hard-pressed to develop a counterprogram for peace in order to defend themselves from the charge that their position was wholly negative and obstructive. There were several efforts to build American plans for peace. The association of nations, the first substitute for the League, proved to be no more than a campaign crutch and failed to satisfy the public's desire for effective peace machinery. Next the Republican administration of Harding and Hughes represented the Washington Conference as the greatest step toward world peace in the bloodstained history of the human race, but this move did not satisfy many Americans anxious for peace.

During these same years, the mid-1920's, many Americans who decried military force sponsored the World Court. It was logical to expect that Hughes, who felt that law rather than force was the civilized approach to international order, would help launch the movement for membership in the Court, the most effective approach to peace consistent with American traditions. Anticipating the inevitable reaction of the Senate, Hughes in submitting the Court's protocol to the Senate drafted four reservations to safeguard American independence of action.

For a brief while there was hope for success. The influential archisolationist, Senator Borah, favored a court—so much so in 1923 that irreconcilables disowned him and looked to Hiram Johnson as head of the isolationist bloc in the Senate. But exile of the senator from Idaho was premature. Borah soon concluded that what masqueraded at Geneva in the guise of a benevolent judicial tribunal was, in fact, a baleful international political tribunal. It could not find separation from the League, he believed, for the Court was identical to the League; it was to the League of Nations as water was to H_2O. Membership in the Court was (to change the figure of speech) the backdoor to League membership. In sum, Borah, the spokesman of a vast body of opinion, did not want to see the United States sacrifice traditions by wandering through any door, however attractive, into a political league based on military power.

Apart from its relation to the League, Borah also saw mechanical weaknesses in the World Court structure. It could not compel nations to submit disputes for review; without such power, he claimed, there could never be a "real" court. Advocates of the Court dismissed Borah's insistence on compulsory jurisdiction, so sharply in contrast with his insistence on complete national sovereignty, as another example of his obstructive technique of opposing any practical approach to peace because it fell short of perfection. But the Lion of Idaho continued to oppose *the* Court and to support *a* court based on what he liked to describe as "affirmative jurisdiction."

This was a utopian plan indeed, for the real issue was to assure Americans that force would not be used by the Court. Secretary of Commerce Herbert Hoover assured the public in 1925 that no political entanglements would result from membership in the Court and that enforcement of its decisions would rest on public opinion, not force. In supporting the Court, he said, the United States would "subscribe to no compulsion whatever." That membership in the court would mean co-operation with the League of Nations or bring the United States into the League as a member through the "back door, side door, or cellar door" was denied by Harding himself. Even such eminent Republican statesmen as these could not dispel fear of entanglement in the affairs of Europe, and John T. Adams, Chairman of the Republican National Committee, found himself compelled to denounce the administration's plan to join the Court. The Republican party, Adams said, still stood with the sixteen million voters who had repudiated European entanglement in 1920; the party would continue to review and discuss political problems from the standpoint of "America First."

Political exigencies and parliamentary guile postponed Senate debate on the World Court until December, 1925. By that time the public's hope that its yearning for peace could be satisfied by the Court had brought an overwhelming popular demand for membership. Based as it was on the rule of law and the process of arbitration, the Court would bring the blessing of peace without guaranteeing the *status quo* in Europe with American military forces. The Court, in the words of many petitions sent to the Senate, would be the first step toward "ultimately outlawing war as a relic of barbarism, a crime, and a direct repudiation of the principles taught by Christ." Many petitioners expressed the hope that settlement of the Court issue would solve all problems of foreign affairs, so that attention could turn to the most important issues facing the country —matters of domestic politics.

The resolution for a membership in the Court hedged by reservations won a Senate majority in 1926, but subsequently the Coolidge administration refused to discuss the meaning of these reservations in conference, as the forty-eight members of the Court requested, and the resulting impasse blocked American membership. The campaign against the Court which Borah had already launched in Chicago proved unnecessary. Speaking there on Washington's Birthday, 1926, he had challenged his listeners: "Shall we exchange the policy which dedicated this country to peace since its foundation, for the policies and practices which have dedicated the continent of Europe to war for a thousand years?"

Still unsatisfied was the demand for a positive program for peace consonant with American traditions. In time this ideal, frustrated in the failure of the court, at last found form in the Kellogg-Briand Pact for the renunciation of war. The treaty was in part a response to the popular demand in the United States by 1928 that war be "outlawed." This movement was largely the work of S. O. Levinson, a wealthy Chicago lawyer, who in 1918 developed a program for peace which included codification of international law, the establishment of a world court, and an agreement by all nations to declare war illegal. At this time he coined the phrase "to outlaw war." The slogan had great popular appeal as did the idea of establishing peace by the simple and inexpensive expedient of declaring war to be abolished. Levinson spent lavishly of time and money to popularize his program and force governmental action through an aroused public demand. In this he sought the support of Senator Borah, an able but reluctant champion, who, partly to delay and partly to perfect the program, raised many questions and made a number of suggestions.

Probably the most important issue raised in drafting the program was that of enforcement. Levinson had begun in 1918 with a theory that outlawry of war must be backed by over-whelming military force. Contact with Senator Philander C. Knox soon convinced Levinson that this program was impracti-cal and undesirable, but no definite alternative to force had de-veloped by 1921, when he first asked Borah to endorse outlawry of war. Borah had assailed use of military force as a part of the League of Nations, and had opposed it as part of the Four-Power Treaty of the Washington Conference. But when faced with the possibility of having to defend the plan of outlawry before the United States Senate, he needed a definite proposal for effective nonmilitary enforcement; and with Levinson he worked on this problem throughout 1922.

During their discussions Levinson insisted that the theory of "preponderance of power or alliances, or any qualities of force" had been removed from his plan in favor of a reign of law obviating the need for an international police force. When all nations condemned war as a crime, responsibility for war could be fixed upon leaders who brought about war. They could be punished by the people of their own nations. In this manner the law would be upheld, but state sovereignty would not yield to the decrees of a superstate. Levinson felt that when war was no longer recognized as a legal method of set-tling disputes, nations, being eager to observe all laws, would not resort to war. These legalistic arguments did not convince Borah, who was practical enough to fear that national interest might override a nation's desire to observe law.

Borah and Levinson's final solution to these questions of nonmilitary coercion was the proposal to establish a "judicial substitute for war," a world court similar to the Supreme Court of the United States. Its powers would not include, in theory or in fact, the right to use force in executing decisions. They would rest on "the compelling power of enlightened public opinion"; the court was to possess "affirmative jurisdiction to hear and decide all purely international controversies as defined by the code, or arising under treaties." In Borah's resolution on outlawry, presented to the Senate February, 1923, this court was the principal method of enforcement. Also included was provision for a "solemn agreement" binding each nation "to indict and punish its own international war breeders or instigators and war profiteers."

Borah and Levinson agreed on elimination of all military force from American diplomacy. They came to believe this the most important feature of their plan, placing it squarely in the American tradition and distinguishing it from the futilities of all European and some American peacemakers.

Paralleling the work of Borah and Levinson was the labor of the Federal Council of Churches. This body in 1924 drafted a treaty declaring that "aggressive war is an international crime," and sent it to the League of Nations with the suggestion that all members sign a treaty to that effect. In the same year a group of Americans including James T. Shotwell, General Tasker H. Bliss, and David Hunter Miller drew up and sent to the League Assembly the "Proposal of the American Group," a Draft Treaty of Disarmament and Security opening with a "Declaration Outlawing Aggressive War." This was its only similarity to the Borah plan. Nations failing to submit disputes to arbitration were to be branded as aggressors and subject to military discipline by other members. The League Committee never discussed the Draft Treaty, but Shotwell later claimed that it was the inspiration of the Geneva Protocol of 1924, a somewhat similar plan adjusted to the special requirements of European politics and based on military sanctions.

Shotwell and his associates in the mid-1920's launched an attempt to unite the peace movement in America on a single outlawry of war program compatible with the Geneva Protocol. This movement, the Harmony Plan, collapsed over the issue of military sanctions. In the plans of Shotwell and his friends there was to be co-operation with the League; military sanctions would be used against aggressor nations. Borah and Levinson, of course, rejected military sanctions and refused to accept any attempt to define aggression. Determining the aggressor would be an impossible task, they argued; nations always went to war for defensive purposes. No progress could be made so long as some types of war were classed as good and others as bad. All wars should be outlawed. As a consequence of this insoluble conflict over military sanctions, the American peace movement remained divided. The Geneva Protocol failed in Europe; the Harmony Plan failed in the United States.

As was frequently the case, Borah in his position on the Harmony Plan once more reflected popular sentiment. Americans were determined to stand free of any commitment to use military force, or any obligation under a set pattern of action in foreign affairs (independent nationalism, as it was sometimes called). Even so, American leaders had to deal with the vague popular notion that co-operation with other nations to achieve world peace was necessary and could be achieved. The Kellogg-Briand Pact of 1928 met all these aspirations of the American people.

Military sanctions were not a part of this plan. The pact's author, Secretary Kellogg, explicitly stated that if a nation violated its pledge not to use war as an instrument of national policy, it would by that act release all other nations from any obligations under the Pact. In the United States this official interpretation found acceptance.

The Shotwell faction in the peace movement had sought to forestall such an interpretation. They hoped their definition of an aggressor would be adopted by Kellogg, who as late as December, 1927, favored sanctions. But Borah, who worked closely with Kellogg in negotiation of the treaty, nullified this work and incorporated in the treaty his opposition to defining an aggressor or linking the agreement with a system of military sanctions. During the late stages of negotiations Kellogg declared repeatedly that the United States could not be a party to any peace plan which "finds its ultimate expression in a resort to arms and perpetuates a system of international alliances." More than anything else it was the belief that peace would be promoted without requiring the sacrifice of traditions that gave the treaty a popular appeal in the United States. After signature of the Pact of Paris, Kellogg wrote Borah: "I know of no moral obligation to apply sanctions or to take affirmative military action in any case, whatever might happen; in fact, this is the only kind of treaty, as you have always said, that we can possibly sign."

Senate debate on the Pact underscored the popular concern lest obligations, explicitly avoided in the text, be implied in its provisions. There was, however, a demand that there be no impairment of the right of self-defense and the right to extend protection to citizens. Some senators charged that the Pact was worthless because it did not provide for military sanctions, but they made no effort to reinforce it in terms of military or economic force during the debate. On the contrary, Senators Reed and Moses, ignoring Borah's eloquent explanation that the treaty was not based on force, proposed a reservation stating that "the United States would not resort to coercive or punitive measures against any offending nation."

To defeat this proposal Borah, as principal Senate champion of the treaty, devoted much time to denunciation of the theory that military force could foster peace. The psychology of peace had to replace the psychology of war. Otherwise even disarmament could not bring peace; the nations would continue to "fight with their fists." The aim was not preventing war, an outworn ideal, but "organizing peace which is a wholly different thing." The Pact of Paris, a bold new approach to peace, was not founded on "the theory of force or punitive measures at any place or at any time."

The Pact, Borah believed, was an end in itself. Other champions of peace, such as Shotwell, saw it as a bridge to the League or to some effective form of collective security. Senator Capper in 1929 introduced a resolution empowering the President to decide in event of war which of the nations involved was the aggressor. President Hoover, soon after taking office, talked with Shotwell and later suggested to Kellogg, then at the end of his term in office, "some stronger diplomatic teeth for the Pact" including an investigative commission to fix responsibility for violations of the Pact, withdrawal of diplomatic recognition from guilty nations, and refusal to recognize their titles to territory acquired by aggression. Kellogg rejected these proposals, as did Ramsay MacDonald when they were discussed with him later in the year.

At the London Disarmament Conference in 1930 a somewhat different approach developed. Unsuccessful efforts were made to gain from the United States agreement to consult with other powers in event the Pact was violated. Stimson, at Hoover's behest, refused these proposals on grounds that agreement to consult implied a moral obligation to execute with armed force the decision reached.

This matter was brought up many times during the next three years. Hoover, for personal as well as political reasons, called a consultative pact an impossibility when the French broached the matter in the autumn of 1931. Outbreak of conflict in Manchuria again inspired the idealism of expediency. There was new talk about consultation and a number of resolutions were introduced in Congress providing for sanctions. When the political conventions met in 1932, both Democrats and Republicans endorsed consultation in their platforms as a means of strengthening the Kellogg Pact. Unlike the Congressional resolutions, the platforms did not assume that consultation would result in action and carefully avoided any reference to the use of sanctions.

In his speech accepting the nomination in 1932, Hoover promised consultation to promote peace. This, he made clear, did not imply an intention "to enter any agreement or follow any course of action calling for the use of force to prevent war." This and other statements caused Admiral Leahy, for one, to

condemn Hoover as "an internationalist" and to support Franklin Roosevelt as a true American and nationalist.   Roosevelt's campaign and his early years in office did not bring
any marked break with the dominant isolationist and pacific
mood of the country.   Popular will continued to dictate policy
down to 1939.   The administration, so its leaders recalled years
later, sought to expand the nation's military forces and thwart
isolationist legislation in order to give authority to foreign
policy and provide security in the event of war.

Judged by accomplishment rather than by these aspirations, the Roosevelt administration followed a policy in keeping with its predecessors in the matter of military force and
foreign policy.   There were, from time to time, suggestions
for a new policy, but they were not followed through.   It
was true, for example, that at the Geneva Conference on
Disarmament of 1933 the administration, through Norman
Davis, announced willingness to go beyond earlier precedents
in consulting with other powers in the interest of peace.   This
might have marked an important departure—the beginning of
a joint military-diplomatic policy—but it was conditioned on a
satisfactory agreement limiting armament.   This important condition could not be met by Europeans.   Furthermore, consultative pacts were a political liability in the United States.

During the year 1935 the growing power of the European
dictators brought the problem of force in foreign policy before
the nation once again: Should the United States co-operate
with the peace-loving European nations?   The administration
urged action of a conservative sort—approval of the World
Court Protocol drafted by Elihu Root in 1929.   Even with
the inevitable Senate safeguards against entangling alliance,
the Court Protocol failed once more.   The vote defeating the
Court was not so much the result of a tidal wave of anti-Court
propaganda that swamped the Senate as it was a reflection of
a well-fixed American determination to remain clear of Europe.

In following years Roosevelt found it much more popular
to "hate war" than to develop a "quarantine of aggressors."
Polls indicated that in the latter 1930's the great majority of

Americans, over 70 per cent, opposed any use of military sanctions in the interest of peace. The New York *Times* in 1938 demanded a policy that would increase the possibility of continued peace, but it stipulated that it must be peace without "the substance or sanctions of war."

The public sentiment of the 1930's, and to a large degree of the entire era between the wars, found an apt illustration in the proposed Ludlow "referendum" on war. Under its terms an amendment of the Constitution would make declaration of war impossible without a majority vote of the people, save only in case of need to repel actual invasion. George Harvey in 1920 had suggested a similar plan to Harding. It was, Harvey maintained, a proposal that dwarfed all other plans for peace. From time to time during the next decade a referendum on war had won minor support. Ludlow's proposal in 1935 gained signatures of fifty-five congressmen and the endorsement of former Secretary Kellogg. Presented to the House of Representatives, it was kept in committee until late 1937. A vote to take it out and place it before the House failed in January, 1938, by the fairly narrow margin of 209 to 188. The administration, according to Cordell Hull, exerted every possible pressure to bring defeat of the Ludlow proposal. Had the popular will prevailed at this point, the measure would have been passed. Polls showed that 80 per cent of the American people favored a referendum on war, and 218 congressmen, prior to the vote, had signed a petition approving it.

This debate illustrated much of the popular philosophy on the place of power in the making of policy. Congressmen argued that there was no danger of invasion. It would take a hundred transports of twenty-knot speed to bring to American shores a dangerous force; no nation had such a fleet. There was no possibility of involvement in European war: "If the old nations of the world go to war, it is their war and not ours," said Hamilton Fish. The only danger, and the referendum on war eliminated it, was that "the United States may be dragged into a war in which she has little, if any, interest."

Even more important was the protection which the referendum provided for the ideals of democracy. It was "an epochal advance in the cause of popular rule"; it held much "hope for the future of democracy." It would banish war from American shores. No accomplishment was more important than this. Democracy could scarcely live in a state of war or a condition of continued preparation for war. The rights of the individual would find protection in the Ludlow referendum: those who would have "to fight and die in war and to bear the indescribable burdens and cost and griefs of war" would decide when they would go to war.

Such, then, were some of the efforts of Americans to maintain in the interwar years a foreign policy divorced from military force. The principal concern of the era was how a civilian democracy might cope with the dangers of building a foreign policy based on military force. In a period of comparative peace, the obvious answer was to protect the civilian democracy by not building a military force.

For a time after the Second World War broke out, there was, among the people and leaders in the United States, a dogmatic conviction that the unwillingness to prepare and use military force in the 1920's and 1930's led to the policy of appeasement bringing in turn the catastrophe of world conflict. Conversely it was assumed that through a world organization backed by force, peace might be secured.

In the 1950's there is less certainty that power and peace are correlative. There still lingers the ideal that brute force even in the name of law is archaic. A rule of law and morality can be established. Indeed, in view of modern weapons of war, it is argued, such a rule must be established. On the other hand, it is maintained that power is a "stubborn social and psychological fact" by which international behavior has always been governed and must continue to be governed.

4. Robert H. Ferrell

The Peace Movement

We highly resolve that these dead shall not have died in vain.
—inscription on the tomb of the Unknown Soldier, dedicated November 11, 1921.

WHAT, BRIEFLY, has been the history of the peace movement in the United States?

One fact is immediately apparent: the heyday of the movement, its era of greatest influence, came during the interwar period. Although the peace movement in America proudly traced its origin to the early nineteenth century, to the years after the Napoleonic wars, its day of influence really began after the World War of 1914-1918. Its history, prior to the First World War, was that of a genteel, blessed, but ineffective reforming movement.

In the century before 1914 there seemed little need for a peace movement. The world was, generally speaking, a peaceful place. Practical humanitarians in the United States gave their attention to such exigent evils as slavery and polygamy. While there was a peace movement in America during the early nineteenth century, it was a highly doctrinaire undertaking, part of the ferment of idealism that produced Transcendentalism and the utopian community schemes. The peace plans of William Ladd and Elihu Burritt, the founding of the Massachusetts Peace Society in 1815, the American Peace Society in 1828—all this was rich in activity but poor in practical effect. It could not halt the Mexican War or dissuade the nation from Civil War. In the years after 1865, American energies turned to railroad building, exploiting the West, industrializing the East. So much peace was there that the peace movement in the United States kept alive only with difficulty. Andrew Carnegie created the Carnegie Endowment for International Peace in 1910, Edward Ginn endowed the World Peace Foundation, and Carnegie in 1913 constructed at The Hague a grand peace palace as a permanent home for the Permanent Court of Arbitration; but these were personal creations, unrepresentative of the broad currents of American thought. The peace movement found few supporters until after the First World War.

It was the World War that gave purpose to the movement. The war of 1914-1918 suddenly fastened the attention of Americans upon the problem of total war, which had never confronted them prior to that time. Our people so hated the bloodshed and material waste of the First World War, so longed for peace during the grim years of the fighting in Europe, that in the era after 1918 avoidance of war and preservation of peace became the central theme of American foreign policy. Concern over war was only heightened when during 1919-1920 there occurred the momentous "slump in idealism" that defeated the Treaty of Versailles and the Covenant of the League of Nations. Today, after nearly forty years, it is difficult to recapture the feeling of intense disillusion, of disgust and revulsion, that attached itself to American memories of the World War within months of the end of the war. Probably President Woodrow Wilson had keyed American emotions too high during the great crusade, and a let-down became inevitable. The people expected too many benefits from the war, and were bound to discover that the world did not wish to abolish secret diplomacy and make itself safe for democracy. For whatever reason, the Milwaukee Socialist, Victor L. Berger, soon was announcing with authority, and found millions of Americans ready to believe him, that all the United States got out of the war was flu and prohibition. This cynicism reinforced the peace movement during the 1920's and 1930's and gave it popular support of a kind that it had never had before. There arose the innumerable private popular organizations devoted to preservation of peace: the League of Nations Association, the Woodrow Wilson Foundation, the American Committee for the Cause and Cure of War, the National Committee for the Prevention of War, the American Committee for the Outlawry of War. Older peace organiza-

tions, such as the Carnegie Endowment and the World Peace
Foundation, took on new life. Wartime organizations, such as
the Woman's International League for Peace and Freedom,
found new reason for existence.

Despite all the frenzied activity of these organizations,
another world war came. The peace movement had failed.
Again it went into eclipse. Ten years and more after V-E
and V-J days, little was being heard from it. Such peace
societies as survived the Second World War became far different groups from what they had been before the war. They
turned their attention to the United Nations, and the Carnegie
Endowment spent most of its available funds constructing a
futuristic Peace Building within a stone's throw of the UN
where, it hoped, all the peace organizations could maintain
offices. The remnants of the once-mighty peace movement
have concentrated themselves along the East River and become, as it were, adjuncts of the United States delegation at
the UN.

So much for the history of the peace movement, a movement which collapsed and died at the beginning of the Second
World War, after two short decades of influence and power.
What can the historian say about this organized campaign
for international peace? Was it simply one more utopian effort
by the gullible American public, an effort bound to break
against the hard facts of international life? Or is there tragedy
in the demise of the peace movement—the tragedy of noble
men and hopes defeated by forces over which they had no
control? What effect did the movement have upon the broad
process of American life and thought? Would the course of
history in this country have been much the same, had there
never been a peace movement? Did the Second World War
come more quickly, or the United States find itself less prepared when the war came, because there was such a strongly
organized movement for peace in the interwar years?

I

To answer the above questions one must discuss, first of
all, the dominant ideas of the American peace movement in

the interwar period—the proposals of the varied groups of private citizens who sought to prevent the recurrence of world war. Several ideas for preservation of world peace received popular attention during the period: the League of Nations, the World Court, disarmament, the Kellogg-Briand Pact, arbitration and conciliation, freedom of world trade, neutrality legislation. None of these gained the complete enthusiasm of all the numerous organizations. Still, if taken together they represent most of the thoughts of the peace movement in the interwar era.

The League of Nations. Here was, of course, the great hope for peace after the First World War. The League of Nations Covenant may not have pulsed to the "heart of the world," and certainly was never the heart of the American peace movement, but the League captured and held for twenty years the support of broad sections of the American "intelligentsia"—the professional classes, especially the teachers and the preachers. These good people did little to assist the formal League of Nations Association. The latter, organized early in 1923 as a reincarnation of the wartime League to Enforce Peace, enrolled in its first months considerably fewer than 50,000 members. Nevertheless, an unnumbered host of Americans found the League a most attractive organization and lamented the failure of the United States to ratify the Treaty of Versailles, which included the Covenant.

The force of the League idea in American thinking on foreign affairs becomes clear after the briefest examination of the literature and statement-making of peace organizations in the 1920's and 1930's. If such organizations did not actually support the League, they frequently (as in the case of the Carnegie Endowment for International Peace) described themselves as "favoring co-operation with the League." Even the peace organizations of less conservative background than the Carnegie Endowment, organizations founded on the idea that any formal connection with a European international body was virtually immoral, could not ignore the League. They had to fight an idea so important in American international thinking, and assert, for instance, that the League's program of peace was in reality a program of war. Opponents of the League often came out in the open in their attacks, especially after the "solemn referendum" of 1920. Sometimes they resorted to subtlety, as did the eminent Protestant clergyman, Charles Clayton Morrison, in a book on *The Outlawry of War: A Constructive Policy for World Peace* (Chicago, 1927). Although Morrison throughout his book referred to "outlawry" as "Outlawry," he insisted upon spelling "League of Nations" as "league of nations."

The League entered into most of the postwar debates over the proper way to maintain peace. Still, Americans in the interwar period failed almost completely to look into the actual working of the League, to see what the League really could have been expected to do. The most perceptive book about the League in the era 1918-1941 was the work of a Britisher, Sir Alfred Zimmern. The books of such American students as Denna F. Fleming and Pitman B. Potter were little more than pro-League tracts, eulogies or unimaginative cataloging of commissions and bureaus. A number of American scholars who might have written intelligent analyses of the League's prospects concentrated their attention on the Senate and denounced it for repudiating the Covenant. Rather than asking themselves what the League could have done for European and world peace in the years after the Paris Conference, they studied the personalities of Senator Lodge and President Wilson. It was, perhaps, a little too easy for scholars to apportion blame for the Covenant's defeat in the United States. It was too easy for the American peace organizations to stand for or against the League on the basis of the relatively unrefined arguments of 1919-1920 projected without much change into the complex world of the 1920's and 1930's. Debate over the League seldom raised important questions like these: How could the League be greater than the sum of its parts? Was it possible to deal with the serious high-political problems of great powers within the frame of the League? Did the Covenant embody that most important of institutional arrangements, a proper linking of the functions of decision and responsibility?

Nowhere did the peace movement show its intellectual limits better than in its activity in regard to the League of Nations. The various private organizations devoted to the cause of peace could never manage to get out of the role of advocate long enough to examine, in a sharply critical manner, the programs on which they took their stands. In the case of the League, the peace organizations chose sides, usually for emotional reasons, and then turned what should have been an intellectual discussion into a debate. For example, Article 10 of the Covenant contained (according to such anti-League organizations as the American Committee for the Outlawry of War) the most dangerous promise that the United States could ever undertake: a guarantee of the boundaries of every nation in the world. Pro-League organizations hotly denied this. No one apparently bothered to read with care the exact wording of Article 10, to observe the several qualifications which made it no more than a harmless statement of good will. "The Members of the League," so ran the article, "undertake to respect and preserve as against external aggression the territorial integrity and existing political independence of all Members of the League." Nowhere in this declaration did the word "guarantee" occur.

The article bore a marked similarity to John Hay's Second Open Door Note of 1900, which provided for preserving the territorial and administrative entity of China. At the turn of the century John Hay's note had seemed a diplomatic triumph; twenty years later a similar pledge was considered to endanger American independence. There were, of course, practically no dangers in the other articles of the Covenant, but under the influence of the arguments of 1919-1920 the smallest possible commitment to world peace became fraught with difficulty. The peace movement could have performed a useful service in this matter if it had disentangled fact from fancy and lifted the League debate to a plane of reasoning. Somehow this was impossible, perhaps because the peace movement was so intensely "activist," so much a promoting movement rather than an agency for information and thought. As a result, the issue of the League of Nations, first in importance of the several programs championed by peace organizations, never received the intelligent discussion that it deserved. The entire League debate was a frustrating affair, and when as a political issue it gave way in the later 1920's to the issue of Prohibition, there was less of a change from the serious to the nonserious than some individuals believed.

The World Court. Like the League, the World Court upon its creation in 1920 quickly became an article of faith to many Americans, and peace organizations of the interwar period usually felt called upon to make statements about it, pro or con. The World Court, more than any other idea for preserving peace, enjoyed general favor in the United States. Even such confirmed anti-League men as Senator William E. Borah found the idea attractive. Unfortunately, when the Court's connection with the League—its duty to give advisory opinions upon request of the League—proved its undoing, so far as concerned acceptance by the Senate, peace organizations found themselves altogether unable to guide American opinion, despite their liking for the idea of a court. They could not detach themselves long enough from the League debate to judge the World Court on its merits. Senator Borah, who supported many anti-League peace organizations, found it necessary to come out in favor of a world court aseptically clear of League contamination; it was not easy to discover a substitute court that differed in any major respect from the World Court, but Borah managed to give the impression that he had developed a "real" court. Possessing a genius for capturing the moral fervor of America, without the slightest ability to guide that fervor in any practical direction, Borah in twenty years of speeches and conversation kept to his vague ideal of a world court, meanwhile doing much to prevent American ratification of the court already in existence. Having entangled himself in the League debate, he could not judge impartially even a remotely connected issue.

It was probably because of the legal background of American life itself—the heritage, through American history, of Calvinism, Coke, and the federal Constitution—that the idea of a court, whether in the form of World Court or world court, carried appeal for American peace groups. Americans had far more faith in the possibilities of international law than did Europeans. Secretaries of state frequently made glib comparisons between municipal and international law: the two systems were supposedly the same in essence, i.e., federal; to make international law function as easily and well as municipal law, one had only to create an international court. That the two kinds of law were quite different was seldom understood. It was in vain that such international lawyers as Edwin M. Borchard pointed out the peculiarities of international law—the concern of the law of nations with rules for war (international lawyers usually divided their treatises into two equal sections, the law of war and the law of peace). To no avail Borchard would indicate the effectiveness of international law in small matters like the immunities of ambassadors or the mechanics of ratifying a treaty, and its ineffectiveness and confusion in larger matters like neutral rights and duties. The peace movement in advocating a world court might well have studied the essential differences between municipal and international law, to see how those differences would limit any international juridical body. They could have seen that the World Court was established with such timidity that its Protocol expressly stipulated that the Court's decisions would not have the effect of setting precedents—that the League Court could not even cite the authority of its own decisions. Instead of examining into the difficulties of international law and the restricted nature of the World Court, the peace movement again, as in the case of the League, mirrored American opinion rather than informed it.

Some American peace workers advanced incredibly obtuse arguments in favor of a court. Salmon O. Levinson of Chicago, who in 1921 had set up the American Committee for the Outlawry of War, was absolutely convinced that a court would assure world peace. Levinson did take his conviction back one step to the necessary codification of international law; but he saw no difficulty on that score: he thought that codification of international law was a simple procedure, requiring two, perhaps three years of work by an international conference. The code, he said, should be "comprehensive." In it "the wisdom of the ages should be distilled and all good things that have been developed in international law should be preserved and the evil cast out." Once completed, the code would be submitted "to each civilized nation and be by it approved. As each of such nations will participate in the preparation of the code, general harmony may be expected." Actually, there has been no ratified codification of international law since 1907; and much of what was codified before then has since been shot to pieces.

The idea of a world court, or the World Court, like the idea of the League of Nations, never really came under studious scrutiny of peace groups in the interwar period, despite the close interest of such statesmen as Elihu Root, who devoted his final years to seeking acceptance of the World Court. People believed that if Senator Borah, who had never traveled outside of the continental United States, mentally or physically, said that the nations needed a world court, then that was what the nations needed. There was almost no criticism of the world court idea as a practical measure in international affairs; the World Court, like the League of Nations, became a matter for emotional rather than for logical discussion.

Disarmament. Another approach to peace which had currency in the interwar years was disarmament. This idea stemmed largely out of the experience of the World War. In looking for causes of the war, Americans and many Europeans noted the size of European armaments prior to 1914. Though aware of other causes, these people believed that the piling up of armaments in Europe had made hostilities inevitable. Armaments, they reasoned, had become so large by 1914 that the smallest spark, the smallest diplomatic crisis, could and did result in an enormous explosion.

The idea of disarmament had flourished somewhat even before the World War, though far less extensively than it did afterward. The Tsar of Russia, at the request of his minister of finance, Count Serge Witte, had convened at The Hague in 1899 a large international conference which gave attention to disarmament. The Tsar's idealism developed after Witte pointed out that France, Germany, and Austria-Hungary were equipping their armies with a new type of field gun, the so-called "French 75," which the Russian treasury would be unable to purchase and at the same time finance some necessary new warships. Count Witte, preferring the new warships, hoped that the Tsar could obtain at The Hague a moratorium of 75's in the name of disarmament and world peace. But the other world powers were aware of these Russian motives and nothing came of disarmament. In later years the idea languished, for as Sir Edward Grey told the House of Commons in 1907, "The difficulty in regard to one nation stepping out in advance of the others is this, that while there is a chance that their courageous action may lead to reform, there is also a chance that it may lead to martyrdom."

After the war disarmament not only gained large popular favor in Europe and America, but also acquired a certain practicality, especially in regard to reduction of naval strength. With the German fleet destroyed, Great Britain and the United States had less need to retain large naval armaments. The Japanese government was uncertain of the feasibility of disarmament; yet, under the force of an American threat to outbuild the Japanese Navy, Japan agreed at the Washington Naval Conference of 1921-1922 to accept the short end of a 5-5-3 ratio for battleships and aircraft carriers. At the London Naval Conference in 1930 this ratio, with some modifications, was extended to include auxiliary naval craft.

Peace organizations in the United States during the 1920's, the heyday of disarmament, enthusiastically endorsed the incautious statement in Sir Edward Grey's memoirs, published in the mid-1920's, that "great armaments lead inevitably to war. . . . The enormous growth of armaments in Europe . . .

made war inevitable." They believed that everyone who worked against disarmament was *ipso facto* a "militarist," of the sort that had caused the World War. They believed that national armies as well as national navies should be limited or reduced in size, although they readily admitted that the United States, possessing a minuscule army, must make its main contribution toward disarmament by limiting its navy. They failed to realize that when they began talking of disarmament in regard to armies, rather than navies, they necessarily struck at the French Army, the only army of any size in the postwar world. They overlooked the fact that this army was the only European force other than the League which, after 1918, could prevent the resurgence of German military power. When they strove to limit the size of armies while remaining aloof from the League they actually worked to undermine the peace of Europe and the world—the very peace they hoped to promote by disarmament. Even when they agitated for naval limitation and reduction, they harmed their own cause. The chief result of this agitation was a reduction of Anglo-American naval forces. The Japanese Navy, oppressed by financial troubles in Japan at the end of the World War, gained a respite from Western competition, in part because of the treaties, and during the 1930's Japan was able to resume naval construction to the disadvantage of the West.

In measuring the effect of the entire interwar agitation for disarmament, one must, however, be cautious. It can be argued that in the 1920's, when peace seemed secure, there was no longer any need for wartime armaments, and that latter-day critics of disarmament were reading the experience of the thirties back into the quite different twenties. Likewise it is true that during most of the 1930's the American Navy received from Congress all and more than it asked for in the way of appropriations, and that any lag of naval construction by the end of the thirties was more the result of the conservatism of naval leaders than any niggardliness of the public and Congress. Perhaps, too, if there had been no disarmament movement there still would have been naval limitation in the United States, for the country would not have stood for large appropriations during the peaceful 1920's (in the 1930's, as mentioned, the situation changed). Could one say, then, that the disarmament campaigns of the peace movement brought no more limitation or reduction of arms than would have come anyway?

In the complicated intellectual history of twentieth-century America it is difficult to sort out cause and effect, but it does seem that the agitation for disarmament was so insistent, well-organized, vociferous, widespread, that it could not avoid affecting the size of American armaments. There were international naval conferences in 1921-1922, 1927, 1930, 1935-1936, and a World Disarmament Conference in 1932-1934. One of the most effective disarmament lobbyists in Washington, Frederick J. Libby, executive secretary of the National Committee for the Prevention of War, maintained an office directly across Pennsylvania Avenue from the State, War and Navy Building during most of the interwar period, and with an annual budget that frequently exceeded $100,000 he carried on nation-wide campaigns for disarmament. His committee of national organizations like the National Education Association and the YWCA thought nothing of sending out, as it did in January, 1927, 430,000 pieces of antiwar literature. In 1932, during the beginning of the World Disarmament Conference, Libby's group distributed free a "Disarmament Clipsheet" every fortnight to 2,500 daily papers in the country; they sent a mimeographed clipsheet to 5,000 country weeklies; staff members gave 3,000 speeches; the Council sponsored 4,000 local Disarmament Conferences, sending them a considerable part of the 2,615,000 pieces of literature it circulated during the year. The War and Navy departments could hardly have ignored the effect of such campaigns. Although the pacific climate of international affairs during the 1920's, together with the exigencies of the federal budget (President Calvin Coolidge in his inaugural address in 1925 said that "Economy is idealism in its most practical form") helped to dictate some limitation of armaments, still the work of the peace movement did its immeasurable part. While the Navy during the latter 1930's received at least as much as it asked for in appropriations, the fleet was not adequate in 1941. This may have been due to the modesty of naval authorities in asking for money or it may well have resulted from years of skimping, of lack of appreciation and praise from the general public, of timidity engendered by the parrot-call of "militarist" that punctuated all congressional debates over naval appropriations during the twenties and early thirties.

Surely, one can conclude, the peace movement's advocacy of disarmament reflected little hard thinking on the relation of force to foreign policy. It reflected a near-complete misreading of the causes of the World War of 1914-1918. The peace movement thoughtlessly proceeded on the inane assumption that (as the *Survey of American Foreign Relations* for 1927 put it) "We may be confident that decrease in armaments is an indication of stability and peace; the level of armaments is a thermometer which all can read; every reduction means a waning of the war-fever, an approach to the re-establishment of health and peace."

The Kellogg-Briand Pact. Next to disarmament, the most fatuous notion of American peace organizations during the interwar period was that peace could be maintained by renouncing war. This theory flowered in the Kellogg-Briand Pact of 1928, signed at American behest by all the nations of the world except Argentina, Bolivia, El Salvador, Uruguay, Andorra, Morocco, Liechtenstein, San Marino, and Monaco. As Richard N. Current relates in his essay in this volume, the Kellogg Pact stipulated that the nations "renounced" war as an "instrument of national policy" and would settle "all disputes or conflicts of whatever nature or of whatever origin they may be" by peaceful means. The Pact was the crowning achievement of the American peace movement in the interwar period. Despite Secretary of State Frank B. Kellogg's initial and private feeling that peace workers were "a set of— —fools" and "— —pacifists," the peace movement managed to coerce and then convert Kellogg to support the Pact of Paris. For negotiating the Pact the Secretary of State received in 1929 the Nobel Peace Prize. At the time of the Pact's signature there was much private skepticism, especially in Europe, but this did not prevent some American diplomats, notably Kellogg's successor, Henry L. Stimson, from seeking to make the Pact the foundation of American diplomacy.

Unfortunately the Kellogg-Briand Pact was too ethereal a creation, too impossible in terms of practical world politics, ever to have become the foundation of anything. China and Soviet Russia actually began violating the Pact a few days before it was proclaimed by President Herbert Hoover. Although the Sino-Russian dispute eventually quieted down, after some sharp raids into Manchuria by Russian troops, consternation momentarily reigned in the State Department, and Assistant Secretary of State William R. Castle wrote in his diary that the Department's problem was to prevent the Kellogg Pact from looking like thirty cents. The crisis passed in 1929, but in 1931-1933 the Japanese in Manchuria violated the pact with impunity. When during Italy's invasion of Ethiopia in 1935-1936 President Franklin D. Roosevelt reminded Premier Benito Mussolini of Italy's promises under the Kellogg Pact, Mussolini told Roosevelt (as F.D.R. privately put it) to "go to hell."

The Kellogg-Briand Pact was one more illustration of what can only be described as a traditional American liking for pronouncement, for doctrine and dogma. The peace movement, by its nature a doctrinaire movement, was much attracted to formulas officially announced. Perhaps one should make allowance for the fact that the United States in the 1920's had experienced only one world war, and would not develop a healthy skepticism for pledges unbacked by force until after another great war. The Kellogg Pact renouncing war was surely the greatest international gesture ever made by the nations of the world. It may be that in the size of the aspiration, apart from any possible utility, there is a certain grandeur. Even so, maintenance of international order after the First World War was a large task in which there was little time for absent-minded gestures, and insofar as the peace movement in the latter 1920's deflected American attention toward outlawry and renunciation of war it actually hindered the vital business of peace.

Arbitration and Conciliation. In the interwar years the ideas of arbitration and conciliation enjoyed enough currency, and actual precedent, that they deserve mention in any analysis of the ideas of the peace movement. The nations of Europe by 1914 had concluded among themselves a hundred or so arbitration treaties, but when diplomats began consulting their national interests in the crisis of that year, no one thought seriously of using them. Americans realized in the postwar years that the usual treaties of arbitration and conciliation contained loopholes —the treaties of arbitration, for example, excluded all questions affecting the vital interests, independence, or national honor of the contracting states, or disputes involving third parties. In other words, the United States and other nations signatory of such treaties refused to arbitrate the questions which led to war. The government in Washington hopefully continued in the 1920's and 1930's to make treaties on the above weak formula, which Secretary Kellogg in 1927 changed inconsequentially to exclude questions of domestic jurisdiction or involving third parties, the Monroe Doctrine, or the League Covenant. The United States concluded conciliation treaties under a plan inaugurated by Secretary of State William Jennings Bryan in 1913-1914. The idea of an airtight arbitration treaty, stipulating for compulsory settlement of disputes, never appealed to the American government, nor for that matter to the leaders of the peace movement.

Arbitration and conciliation should be characterized as nineteenth-century peace schemes, continued in the post-1918 world chiefly because governments were uncertain of the public response if such treaties were abandoned. President Theodore Roosevelt once confided to his friend Sir Cecil Spring-Rice that "I only went into them because the general feeling of the country demanded it." No Secretary of State in the 1920's and 1930's dared to declare a moratorium on what, in terms of any important effect on international peace, was a waste of time. There was no point in antagonizing the peace advocates. Moreover, such treaties had a certain diplomatic usefulness, in that they signified in a pleasingly vague way that the United States was eager for international friendship. Likewise, refusal to sign an arbitration or conciliation treaty, or slowness in negotiation, might also indicate diplomatic displeasure. For such reasons every administration from Wilson to Franklin D. Roosevelt concluded arbitration and conciliation treaties, though not a single one of these treaties was ever invoked.

Freedom of World Trade. In the interwar years Americans continued to adhere to their traditional faith in freedom of world trade—in a trade largely unrestricted by tariffs, quotas, and other regulations. The American peace movement frequently championed this path to peace, although the idea of freedom of world trade, like the ideas of arbitration and conciliation, failed to attract the peace movement in the manner of such programs as disarmament and the Kellogg Pact, for it seemed to be a less direct attack on war. The World War had impressed upon Americans the urgency of world peace, the importance of "doing something now," and propositions such as freedom of world trade were essentially long range and incapable of quick results. Governments were reluctant to lower their trade barriers; there were interminable delays; so many interests had to be consulted; so many devious tactics, such as health restrictions, quotas, and currency control, could frustrate tariff agreements. The prospects of world peace through freedom of world trade were so remote that American peace leaders became impatient.

It was nonetheless a tradition of American politics that world peace could be maintained through economics rather than politics. The coming of the Great Depression in 1929 lent plausibility to this view; the Depression turned men's minds, as never before, to economic questions. Whether economics really had obtained primacy over politics is at least doubtful. In the twentieth century the apparatus of state power grew to enormous proportions. If there ever were an economic century, it was the nineteenth. Yet in the twentieth century this belief in the priority of economics over politics flourished—partly, no doubt, because of the new-found political power of Marxism—and Secretary Hull promoted his reciprocal trade agreements program during the 1930's—a program that continued into the 1940's and 1950's. This is not the place to examine the Hull program, for it is considered in another essay of this volume. Still, it is worth observing that one of the peace movement's lesser articles of faith was the possibility of world peace through freedom of international trade.

Neutrality Legislation. Last of the peace movement's ideas for international peace was the idea of neutrality, embodied in the legislation of 1935-1936-1937. Neutrality had been a cardinal proposition of American diplomacy from the foundation of the Republic. But because Wilson's interpretation of neutral rights had taken the nation into the World War in 1917, the legislation of the 1930's, so ardently supported by the peace movement, was an effort to choose in advance of war a pacific set of neutral rights. Americans with their unshakable faith in law sought without success to isolate the United States from war by a legal barrier. One need not stop to investigate the unhistorical proposition that if the "interventionists" had not tinkered with the neutrality legislation it would have fulfilled its purpose of keeping the United States out of war. Congress soon changed the neutrality legislation, during debates that caught the interest of all the nation, but Congress changed it gingerly and under color of national de-

fense, lest the new provisions offend the dominantly "isolationist" peace organizations.

II

So much for the principal ideas championed by American
private organizations for world peace during the years 1918-
1941. It is apparent that these peace organizations sponsored
and supported most of the central ideas of American diplomacy
in the interwar period. They entered into all the grand
debates over foreign policy; frequently they inspired leadership.
It remains, then, to examine briefly the mechanics of this leadership: its organizations, membership, financial support, special
purposes.

Two principal types of peace organizations, which for
lack of better words may be characterized as conservative and
radical, flourished in the United States during the interwar
years. The conservative peace organizations included the
Carnegie Endowment for International Peace, the World
Peace Foundation, the Woodrow Wilson Foundation, and
the League of Nations Association. These conservative groups
were Eastern in origin and membership. They possessed considerable financial strength—the Carnegie Endowment, for
example, having received at its foundation in 1910 a gift of
ten million dollars. As for the other conservative organizations,
the World Peace Foundation began its work in 1910 with a
million-dollar endowment, and the Woodrow Wilson Foundation was created in 1923 with initial contributions of nearly a
million dollars.

The work of these organizations was quite varied, perhaps
because they realized that all kinds of activity could come
under the general heading of peace. The Carnegie Endowment spent annually over half a million dollars sponsoring
such projects as a monthly bulletin, *International Conciliation*,
and International Mind Alcoves in small libraries throughout
the United States. It had a large and highly important pub-
lishing program, subsidizing dozens of volumes on international
law and economics, and sponsoring a monumental *Economic*

and Social History of the World War in over one hundred volumes. It also financed smaller peace organizations in the United States and abroad, conducted a Paris Center for European peace, rebuilt the Louvain Library in Belgium, reconstructed the war-devastated French village of Fargniers-sur-Aisne, endowed university chairs of international relations, financed exchange visits of European and American newspapermen and educators, and advanced codification of international law. The World Peace Foundation spent most of its energies working in favor of the World Court and distributing League of Nations publications in the United States. The League of Nations Association was of course the most active supporter of the League. There was also the Woodrow Wilson Foundation, which worked to perpetuate Wilsonian ideals. Among these groups only the League of Nations Association sought members—most conservative peace organizations had their own means of subsistence. The League of Nations Association, as already mentioned, enrolled well below 50,000 members when it began in 1923.

Then there were the radical peace organizations, in many respects the more interesting if not more important part of the peace movement. Almost all of these organizations were born of the World War. A list of the radical peace groups can scarcely be made, for their names changed constantly. There were perhaps forty of them operating at all times on a national level, and many local groups supplemented the activity of the larger national groups. The very names of these radical peace organizations indicate the hopefulness of their programs: the American Committee for the Outlawry of War, the American Committee for the Cause and Cure of War, the Women's International League for Peace and Freedom, the National Committee for the Prevention of War, the Committee on Militarism in Education, the Fellowship of Reconciliation, the Parliament of Peace and Universal Brotherhood, the Peace Heroes Memorial Society, the War Resister's League, the Women's Peace Society, the World Peace Association.

What was their membership and how were these radical groups financed? The American Committee for the Outlawry of War was a small group, financed chiefly by its mentor, Salmon O. Levinson, who spent personally over $15,000 a year to spread the idea of making war illegal. The Women's International League for Peace and Freedom had as many as 6,000 members and some thousands of dollars each year for expenses, much of it provided by friends of the League's founder, Jane Addams. The National Council for Prevention of War had no individual membership, being a federative organization; it often spent over $100,000 a year; in 1928 its roster of full-time workers included twelve secretaries and eighteen office assistants. As for other groups, the Women's Peace Society had 2,000 members, the Fellowship of Reconciliation 4,500, the War Resister's League 400; the finances of these groups varied from time to time, but were never large.

It becomes clear, from the membership and limited finances of the radical groups, that they were not themselves in any sense mass organizations. The inclination to establish "committees," based on other organizations not specifically interested in peace, reveals the difficulty of organizing a substantial membership; it was far easier to obtain funds from some special donor and then form a committee. As John W. Masland has written, the membership of the radical peace movement was astonishingly small, and within it the core of active full-time peace workers was less than a hundred individuals in Washington and New York. Nonetheless those hundred persons, according to Masland, through a maze of supporting peace groups and interlocking committees, were able to reach out to a total of between forty-five and sixty million Americans. And this connection was not merely theoretical. The radical peace groups had a profound effect upon American public opinion. If they did not create opinion, they certainly crystallized existing attitudes, mobilized them, made them vocal. As Masland wrote in 1940, "They have converted a general prevailing attitude into an effective demand for action on a particular measure at a particular time." This they could do, not because of their own zeal but because after the First World War the word "peace" and the several leading programs for peace held such attraction for the American people.

All the radical peace organizations were out to end war as soon as possible; they were little interested in the more gradual approach sponsored by the conservative groups. Arbitration and conciliation treaties, freedom of world trade, the World Court, and the League of Nations—these ideas held limited attraction for the radical peace groups, which were impatient for peace, restless for the abolition of war. The radicals wished to get the job done immediately. As Mrs. Carrie Chapman Catt, the sponsor of the American Committee for the Cause and Cure of War, told a women's meeting in Cleveland in 1921, the time to cure war was now: "The women in this room can do this thing! The women in this room can do this thing!" The radicals wished to replace what they described as the "war system" with a peace system. This meant eliminating as quickly as possible all traces of militarism— through a policy of disarmament—and it meant also the renunciation and outlawing of war through the Kellogg-Briand Pact.

How did the peace advocates, radicals and conservatives, go about putting pressure on the American government and enlisting American public opinion in support of their respective programs? The conservative peace groups frequently operated through the influence of their highly placed members. These groups found it easier to obtain a private interview with a Secretary of State, or with an undersecretary or perhaps an assistant secretary, than to plan a public campaign to influence the American people and thereby the American government. The conservatives championed what could be known (depending on how one looked at it) as either a direct or an indirect approach. They knew, better than the radicals, that to enlist support for a course of action which a political leader or diplomat considered unwise was a most difficult task, subject to evasion, vague promises, and obfuscation of issues. The conservative peace men knew also that the world moved slowly and that it was best to approach public officials with cautious proposals advanced quietly, in hope that so sensible an approach would gain real support.

Such were not the tactics of the radical peace workers, who were too impatient to move slowly, quietly, and indirectly. The radical organizations, born out of fear of a second world war, constantly remembered the danger of gas warfare, which was the bugaboo of the 1920's, or of indiscriminate bombing of cities, the leading fear during the 1930's. They knew that time was important; the militarists, ever lurking in the background, might soon gain power. Zeal drove the radical peace workers to action.

Their organizations employed every device known to the new science of public relations, in an effort to make congressmen and diplomats sense the importance of American measures for world peace. These agitators were adept at the special American device of the fancy letterhead: using as many important names as possible; listing important institutions with which those names had the slightest connection; citing co-operating organizations; boasting of European affiliations; flaunting an ecumenical name, such as the Women's Peace Union of the Western Hemisphere. Then there was the science of placing pressure on government officials, especially congressmen. In such work Mrs. Carrie Chapman Catt was an expert; as she warned one of her workers, she never believed a senator's attitude was sincere unless he became an all-out advocate—unless he had been interviewed by several people and had said the same thing to each one. Along with this science of committing congressmen was the ancillary art of petition-presenting. In accord with the constitutional privilege of all Americans to present petitions to their political representatives, the radical peace workers were constantly inundating congressmen with petitions. The workers early learned that it was advisable to make each letter appear different, even if it were for the same purpose and said the same thing; the technique was to have separately written appeals, individually signed, for these gave the impression in Washington that the agitation of the moment was widespread and not merely the effort of a few people with restricted ideas and unlimited paper.

Most successful of all techniques of the radical peace agitators was that of representing to Congress the female voters of America. This was the favorite technique of Mrs. Catt. The nineteenth amendment to the Constitution had gone into effect shortly after the war, and during the 1920's there was deep concern among political leaders as to how the women of the United States would vote. Precautions were taken, and each of the two major political parties established women's auxiliaries and nominated women vice chairmen of the national committees. Even so, there was fear that somehow the women of America would unite in such a way as to upset the traditional American political balance. The ladies had already done this, to the consternation of male America, by adopting the eighteenth amendment—and who knew what they would do next?

In retrospect it has become obvious that woman suffrage in the United States has made little if any difference except to double the vote. In the 1920's this was not clear, and Mrs. Catt, claiming to represent through her Committee for the Cause and Cure of War the eleven largest women's organizations in the country, was an unknown political quantity, and received respect when she came to Washington to urge the cause of world peace. Generally, one can add, all the radical peace organizations, which were to a considerable extent women's organizations, received far more attention than their actual influence merited, because of this fear that radical peace workers had some special control over the female vote.

As time went on, during the interwar years, the complexion of peace organizations, radical and conservative, changed considerably. It is, in fact, difficult to characterize the peace movement during the last years of the 1930's, for the movement split badly over what became the leading issue of American foreign policy—collective security versus isolation. Each new international crisis in Europe brought increasing urgency to the great debate, and the entire nation took sides. Con-

servative peace organizations took the side of collective security.   The radicals moved, many of them even nearer than
in the past, to the side of isolation.   A number of new peace
organizations appeared, generated not so much because of
memory of the First World War as fear of a second; there
were such novel groups as the Keep America Out of War Congress, Youth Committee against War, Emergency Peace Campaign, America First Committee, and the Committee to Defend
America by Aiding the Allies.   Some of the new groups favored
collective security, some were against it, some could not make
up their minds which way to turn.   As other essays in this present volume show, discussion was never clearly drawn as between
isolation and collective security.   Those two poles seldom found
any adherents at all, for debate circled around such questions as How much collective security? or How much isolation?
The pendulum of general American opinion swung toward
the side of isolation, in hope of keeping America at peace,
until that hope vanished with the attack on Pearl Harbor.

III

What can one say, in conclusion, about the peace movement
in the United States in the period 1918-1941?   Certainly the
results of organized private American efforts for peace during
the interwar years, the results of the peace movement's leadership of American popular sentiment, in no sense corresponded
to the hopes.   There were only superfluous international acts
such as the Kellogg-Briand Pact and the "profuse spawn"
(to use the words of a senator during a congressional debate)
of arbitration and conciliation treaties, together with the highly
dubious achievements in limitation of naval arms at the Washington and London conferences.   If by some curious *ex-post-
facto* operation these treaties and agreements could have been
excised from American and world history during the interwar years, the course of international relations would hardly
have been worse, and without the effects of naval disarmament
it might have been better.

The peace movement went wrong in its ideas. The League, the World Court, disarmament, the Kellogg-Briand Pact, arbitration and conciliation, freedom of world trade, neutrality legislation—none of these, nor all of them together, could have insured international peace after 1918. Perhaps, if some of the conservative peace ideas such as the League of Nations and freedom of world trade had been adopted by the United States early in the 1920's and advanced with a sense of thoughtful concern and unstinted responsibility, and if American diplomacy and military power had worked together in maintenance of peace throughout the world, there might have been a better outcome than the Second World War. Unfortunately the peace movement proved intellectually incapable of fitting its ideas to the facts of international life after 1918. Government officials knew that several of the peace movement's notions were utterly impractical and that in regard to the other ideas there was a broad confusion of counsel among peace workers. American diplomats themselves thought of little that the United States could do, other than exhort, to assist in maintaining peace in Europe and Eastern Asia. They therefore followed no policy at all—which was known as a policy of isolation.

5. *William R. Allen*

Cordell Hull and the Defense of the Trade Agreements Program, 1934-1940

As in [1933] I faced the stupendous problems to be dealt with abroad, it gave me some relief and greater confidence to feel that I was strongly grounded on the fundamental propositions that should govern relations among nations.

CORDELL HULL, 1948

CORDELL HULL, during his quarter century in Congress and then as Secretary of State, centered his approach to foreign policy on the consideration of international commercial relations. The Reciprocal Trade Agreements Program, inaugurated in 1934, was in large measure Hull's creation, and it has been the vehicle of much of American foreign policy during the past two decades. In an evaluation of policies and ideas concerning economic aspects of United States foreign relations in the interwar period, the Trade Agreements Program and its public defense are of high importance.

Here we are concerned primarily with the central strand of the "intellectual history" of the Program—the inclinations and the approach, the mode of analysis and the perspective of Secretary Hull. The purpose of this essay is not to recount the political and economic history of American commercial policy during the years in question, but rather to determine how a distinguished public official considered certain elemental theoretical issues—what economic theories he advanced and how effectively, from the economist's point of view, he formulated them.

Since the first decade of the nineteenth century, the "tariff issue" has been one of the most pervasive elements of American political strife. Supposed differences—which frequently have

been greater than actual differences—on trade and tariff philosophy have been one of the chief criteria in distinguishing
the two major parties.   Moreover, the United States has been
one of the leading trading nations through most of its history, and the tariff, almost from the beginning, has played
a conspicuous part in United States foreign relations.   Especially from the Civil War to the Great Depression, tariff
policy has furnished a revealing reflection of the philosophy
of American foreign policy.   Yet the question may be raised
as to what extent and in what manner it has been an issue in
the minds of public leaders with respect explicitly to *foreign*
policy in general.

In political, as in economic, analysis it is legitimate and
typically necessary to employ a "partial" approach, in which
some significant real-world variables are conceived analyti-
cally to be constants.   Different variables may be held constant in different analyses, and sometimes it is appropriate to
put commercial policy into the other-things-remaining-un-
changed category.   The maker of foreign policy and his historian, however, do well not to relegate international economics
permanently to the class of variables held constant.   There
is more to foreign policy than the political and military considerations of power and security.

Congressmen and other public leaders often, perhaps typically, have attempted to look upon tariff policy as solely a
domestic issue.   Implications of tariff policy with respect to
general foreign relations frequently have been regarded as
nonexistent or so inconsequential as to warrant ignoring them.
Indeed, some statesmen have made it something of a point
of honor to determine their position on the tariff partly with
the touchstone that what would cause consternation in foreign
capitals must surely be optimum policy for American welfare.

Such an attitude toward trade and the tariff does not proper-
ly consign their consideration to the category of purely "domestic" policy.   International trade—regardless of the attitude
toward it and of the philosophy with which commercial policy

is formulated—is a component of international relations. But there remains a distinction between rationally and irrationally constructed foreign policies. American tariff policy has been framed typically by men knowing little and disinclined to learn more about the principles of economics. As a rule, to the questions of commercial policy, there have been given either bad answers or bad reasons in support of good answers.

That the Trade Agreements Act was an improvement over the tariff legislation of, say, the 1920's, few economists would deny; that the act was passed and the Program was supported on an impressive intellectual basis is less apparent. This study of the rationale of the Program, as presented publicly by Cordell Hull in the New Deal era, may suggest that the Program was better than its defense. Nevertheless, the considerable influence of Hull on modern American foreign economic policy has been, on balance, fortunate. Hull was not an economist, but his long-held views were stated with a cogency and a clarity uncommon in public tariff debates.

I

Evaluation requires criteria. Before viewing and weighing Hull's public arguments, it is best to survey basic aspects of international trade theory, of economic interpretations of war, and of the Trade Agreements Act.

International Trade Theory and Commercial Policy. The prospect of mutual gains to the parties in an exchange of goods, services, and claims is the major motivation of market-oriented economic activity, and the conclusion that such mutual gain is possible under certain and typical circumstances is the crux of economic theory. When two bargaining units place different relative valuations on things they possess, there is a range of exchange ratios, or prices, within which trade will benefit each unit. Similarly, when two communities have adjusted their respective consumption and production patterns in such a fashion as to result in different sets of relative prices, they can each profitably trade.

With the emergent possibility of trade between these parties, it is a short step to the principle that specialization in production, partial or complete, can increase the total of goods and services available for trade and consumption. The "law of comparative advantage" holds that a producing unit should specialize in those commodities in which is is *relatively* most efficient.

With each community specializing according to the principle of comparative advantage and exchanging on the basis of such production specialization, each tends, first, to achieve the highest level of "well-being" commensurate with a given aggregate quantity and initial international distribution of goods, and second and simultaneously, to maximize desired output within the constraints of given resources and production techniques. Trade changes the allocation of productive resources, increases world production, and frees nations from the restriction of consuming only their own particular outputs.

The essence of the argument for international specialization and trade, then, is that in this manner a nation may acquire more goods and services than would be possible by itself producing directly with domestic resources all that it consumes.

Economists have typically been champions of substantially free trade. But modern theory does not assert unequivocally that free trade is the only economically rational commercial policy. Free trade can, indeed, contribute to efficiency in the allocation of the world's resources. But a particular nation in the world economy, like an individual producer in the national economy, *may*, under certain circumstances and especially in the short run, gain by appropriate interferences with trade. A protectionist policy, although suspect from the perspective of the global economy, *may* be quite rational from the viewpoint and the typical criteria of an individual country. While under appropriate and common conditions *some* trade is preferable to *no* trade for a country, *restricted* trade may be better than *free* trade for that country. The world is a complicated place—more complicated than one might suppose from listening to United States public tariff debates.

Many specific "economic" arguments, of varying degrees of intellectual respectability, have been offered in the defense of trade barriers. Three are of special relevance to the topic of this paper. (*a*) One ancient and still interesting case is the support of "infant" industries. By receiving temporary protection, a "young" industry may be enabled to realize its potential, develop into a position where it can survive the rigors of unfettered world competition, and perhaps further diversify the economy. In public tariff debates in the United States during much of the period prior to the First World War, this was probably the most prominent line of thought of the protectionists. (*b*) Another hoary but intellectually quite uninteresting defense of protective policies stems from alleged fear of "pauper labor" abroad. In its crudest and most popular form, the argument holds that domestic producers cannot compete with foreign industries if wage rates in the latter are lower than American rates. But neither the wage rate nor the total wage bill is a reliable indicator of total costs per unit of output, which here is the important cost measure. Nevertheless, the "pauper labor" argument remains conspicuous. (*c*) In recent years the development of national income theory has indicated the nature of the relationship between changes in trade and capital flows and changes in the level of economic activity. Money national income is determined by expenditure on current national output, and, other things remaining the same, the development of an export balance will increase the value of equilibrium national income. This conclusion is sufficiently obvious intuitively that the possible effects of increased exports on money national income furnished the basis for much of the tariff debates of the 1930's.

Modern economists are probably less inclined than economists were a generation ago to espouse a doctrinaire position in advocacy of free trade. But even now they are typically reluctant to promote policies of trade restriction. Such concessions from their conventional position as they are willing to make are expressed more readily to each other than to congressional committees and to chambers of commerce.

There are strong reasons for hesitancy in publicly advocating barriers to trade, even though theory suggests that they might sometimes be appropriate according to certain criteria. First, there are complex problems in noting when the prerequisite conditions for imposing restrictions actually exist, in judging whether these conditions will hold for a long enough period to warrant the cost of levying restrictions, in choosing the most appropriate modes of restriction, in determining and administering the optimum degree of restriction, and in maintaining sufficient flexibility to modify the program as conditions change.

Furthermore, there is the general fear that the conclusions of abstract and sophisticated analysis will be expropriated and abused—sometimes deliberately—by persons who are poorly equipped and little inclined to appreciate the limitations of the analysis. Also, without denying possible beneficial effects of trade barriers, it may be that those desired results can be obtained by preferable alternative methods. The outstanding case in point with respect to the tariff debates of the 1930's is possible expansionary income effects of increased exports or curtailed imports, for there are better ways to stimulate national income than by encouragement of an export balance. Finally, policies of trade curtailment which might give a nation certain advantages if it is the only country following such policies will be partially or wholly offset by retaliation. Commercial warfare, an unhappy characteristic of the 1930's, tends to nullify relative gains among countries and to make every nation absolutely worse off.

Trade Theory and the Economic Causes of War. Few would deny that there are "economic causes" of war. More specifically, international trade and finance—or some perversion of international economic relations—may be associated with the emergence of war. But it is not clear that we can *generalize* such contentions into a comprehensive and valid *theory*.

Some have contended that war is always the consequence of something economic—economic circumstances, economic policies, economic motivations. There is the Marxist economic theory of the cause of war, holding that mature capitalist economies generate surpluses of commodities, population, and capital. In the international struggle to export these surpluses, war results.

A somewhat different approach has been dubbed the "scandal" theory. Supposedly war is the result of machinations employed and pressures exerted by nefarious capitalists who anticipate profits from wartime activity.

On the whole, neither the sweeping "surplus" theory of inevitable war nor the simple "scandal" theory of manipulated war is very satisfactory.

Economists generally do not advance propositions concerning the economic causes of war with great confidence. Certainly they are reticent to assign the *sole* causal role in the determination of war to "economic factors." Economists do have much to say about international trade. But trade theory is concerned largely with "the gains from trade," and gains accrue to *both* parties in the transaction. However, political-military strategy may make infliction of injury a goal of national policy. International trade theory, developed, amended, and elaborated over two centuries, is a very impressive intellectual structure. But it is a structure designed to encompass few considerations of "noneconomic" power.

The distinguished economist, Jacob Viner, has contended that war is a product "of the organization of peoples into regionally segregated political groups—in the modern age, in the form of nation-states; of the awareness on the part of each of these groups of the existence of other groups; of the existence of contacts of various kinds between these groups; and of the emergence from these contacts of conflicts of interest." It is to be emphasized that these are not conflicts of solely economic interest: "every kind of human interest which looks to the state for its satisfaction and which involves real or supposed conflict with the interests of other peoples or states is a possible source of contribution to war."

To reject the notion of the exclusively economic causation of war is not to deny that there are so-called economic causes of war. Nor is it to deny that there are possible economic gains from war—which conceivably may be, but probably will not be, greater than associated economic costs. These gains center on international movements of commodities, capital, and people. The victorious nation, in addition to collecting tribute, may either abolish adverse foreign restrictions on such movements or establish restrictions favorable to itself. Both the actual economic consequences of, and the fears, jealousies, and irritations engendered by, foreign-imposed controls will probably be increased if the restrictions are adversely discriminatory. Conversely, gains from applying restrictions against the rest of the world may be enhanced by discriminations of various sorts.

Viner suggests that free trade might be conducive to peace—but not primarily because of its probable contribution to world prosperity or its sometimes supposed inducement to feelings of affection and respect among trading partners. Rather, free trade would increase economic interdependence among nations and thus make war more hazardous; it would increase the costs and inconveniences of disruption of trade by war; it would reduce the economic rationale of aggrandizement for purposes of defense against foreign-imposed hurtful discriminations.

It may be added that the lower trade barriers are, the greater is the reliance on relatively impersonal, as well as relatively efficient, market forces in the allocation of resources. International economic adjustment mechanisms which are alternatives to the free market are likely to involve direct government interferences of a discriminatory and capricious nature. This sort of internationally unco-ordinated, technically clumsy, and perhaps aggressively motivated interference, once started, tends to become cumulative, with acts of one government begetting retaliations and then counterretaliations.

Hull emphasized, as we shall see, an alleged significant contribution which international trade in general and the Trade

Agreements Program in particular could make to the preservation of peace. To what body of concepts and principles and to what collection of analytical techniques can we repair in testing such assertions? Some useful, but limited, observations can be made; some reasonable, but partial, judgments can be passed. These observations and judgments are favorable to unrestricted commerce. But, unfortunately, there is not at present an economic theory of peace and power which is comparable, either in formal elegance or as a tool of conditional prediction, to the economic theory of international trade.

The Trade Agreements Act: An Innovation in American Tariff History. While the "height" of the tariff has followed something of a cyclical variation over the years, there was a strong secular upward trend, especially after the Civil War, until the beginning of the Trade Agreements Program.

The early period of 1789-1816 showed a gradual and steady rise in the tariff, but with major emphasis on customs revenue. From 1816 to 1832 there was a significant increase in rates, with the tariff becoming a major political issue and an avowed national program of protection being widely accepted. During the three decades 1832-1861, with the exception of the years 1842-1846, the tariff gradually fell, and the level of duties just prior to the Civil War reached the pre-1816 level. But 1861-1913 was a long period of a high war tariff and its maintenance, culminating in still higher protection under the acts of 1890, 1897, and 1909. The significance of the relatively low tariff of 1913-1921 was lost in the turmoil of the First World War. With the acts of 1921, 1922, and 1930, the United States formulated a commercial policy of "normalcy" by boosting protection to record heights.

Thus generally for a century and a half, and particularly during the seventy-odd years preceding 1934, the United States employed an illiberal commercial policy. With the three postwar tariff acts, "economic isolationism" achieved new heights, or degenerated to new lows—congressmen, though scarcely economists, differed somewhat on the interpretation, but this is not to deny that Democrats as a group were only a little less protectionist than their Republican brethren. Then the world in general, and the United States more than many countries, became enmeshed in history's most awesome depression, and, typically, arguments for increased restrictions on foreign trade—on imports, that is—have been most cordially received in periods of economic stagnation and decline.

President Franklin D. Roosevelt did not act in a manner to give much encouragement to those like Hull who wished a reversal of America's traditional tariff policy. He did not speak consistently on the tariff issue in the 1932 campaign. In his inaugural address he almost ignored foreign affairs, making an innocuous reference to the intent of being a good neighbor and pointedly observing that "Our international trade relations, though vastly important, are in point of time and necessity secondary to the establishment of a sound national economy. I favor as a practical policy the putting of first things first." Prominent men in the early years of the administration like Raymond Moley and George N. Peek were almost diametrically opposed to Hull on foreign-trade policy. To Hull's disappointment, the President did not include a trade agreements bill in the rush of legislation during the spring of 1933. And then immediately he assumed the role of agent of destruction in the London Economic Conference debacle.

All in all, the passage of the Trade Agreements Act in June, 1934, might well give pause to those who propound the "logic" or "necessity" of history and claim the high predictability of events.

The act instituted a program of bilateral executive commercial agreements to achieve reciprocal reductions in tariff duties and amelioration of other trade restrictions, based on the unconditional most-favored-nation principle, primarily for the promotion of United States exports. It was enacted "for the purpose of expanding foreign markets for the products of the United States," mainly in the interests of combating "the present economic depression." In order "that foreign markets will be made available," it is necessary to afford "corresponding market opportunities for foreign products in the United States," although "the admission of foreign goods . . . [must be] in accordance with the characteristics and needs of various branches of American production."

If the President found duties or other restrictions, domestic or foreign, "unduly burdening and restricting" our foreign trade, he was authorized to enter into trade agreements. No existing rate or duty was to be altered by more than 50 per cent, and generally all concessions made, except in agreements with Cuba, would be extended to all other countries. The "flexible-tariff" provision of the 1930 act, embodying the infamous "cost-equalization" principle which acts to eliminate the basis of trade, was not to apply to articles affected by trade agreements.

The Trade Agreements Program has been administered through an interdepartmental organization representing government departments and agencies concerned with foreign economic policy. While the agreements are effectuated by executive order under congressional authority, such orders do not require subsequent congressional action.

There are few abrupt turns or sudden changes in history. Certain basic principles underlying the Trade Agreements Act were separately adopted in legislation from 1890 to 1930, although they were refined and combined for the first time in the 1934 legislation. These include: (a) tariff negotiations by executive agreement (acts of 1890 and 1897)—although the reciprocity provisions of the 1890 act, based upon penalties rather than concessions, differed materially from the approach stipulated in the Trade Agreements Act; (b) congressional delegation to the President of power to adjust the tariff within prescribed limits (acts of 1922 and 1930); and (c) unconditional most-favored-nation treatment, which was adopted in 1922-1923.

During the first three years of the Program, sixteen agreements were concluded. In 1937 the act was renewed, and during the period 1937-1940 seven more agreements were negotiated. Only four agreements went into effect as long as four years prior to the outbreak of the Second World War in 1939. Obviously the operation of the Program was only well begun when war came. But while it is difficult to evaluate the operation of the Program in the 1930's, plentiful evidence is available on its public defense. We turn now to Hull's trade and tariff position in these critical years.

II

In the spring of 1934 the House Ways and Means Committee and the Senate Finance Committee conducted hearings on the trade-agreements bill. In the presentation of the administration's case, Secretary Hull laid out the general field of discussion and submitted the basic rationale of the proposal.

The first task was to present the plan, seemingly with great reluctance, as "an emergency measure to deal with emergency panic conditions" which were "unprecedented." "Its support is only urged as an emergency measure to deal with [an] . . . emergency situation." Since the proposal was only an antidepression measure, he had to concede that it was also essentially a temporary policy.

Hull's train of thought was, first, that the cause of the panic was the development of "surplus production"; second, that basically domestic measures for recovery, while essential, must be supplemented by increased foreign trade—at least, increased exports—in order profitably to dispose of these surpluses; and third, that the only acceptable method by which to stimulate foreign trade was embodied in the trade agreements bill. He made no significant effort to analyze the causal relationships (as contrasted to assertions of correlation) between "surpluses," international trade, and domestic income and employment. He held simply that the United States has "surplus-producing capacity," that extreme obstructions to trade "inevitably result in . . . constant over-production," and that therefore it is necessary to "supplement our almost impregnable domestic markets with a substantial and gradually expanding foreign market for our more burdensome surpluses."

Only incidentally did he mention to the congressional committees the influence of commerce on peace and of trade restrictions on international friction and war. He presented a more substantial reference to the economic foundations of domestic political developments, expressing the opinion that the cause of antidemocratic revolutions was mainly economic insecurity and poverty.

The Secretary emphasized that the United States should not "underestimate the prestige and influence this nation has" and that it should take the initiative in support of liberalized commercial policies. Far from being in a position to assume world leadership in commercial practices, the United States was losing its relative share of total trade, Hull insisted, because of lack of bargaining procedures as flexible as those of other nations. Foreign powers had no inclination to attempt to negotiate trade agreements with the United States because of its cumbersome methods, particularly after the failure to ratify the Kasson treaties negotiated under the Act of 1897. The American executive should receive authority "somewhat on a parity" with that of other executives to deal effectively with trade problems. Hull was confident that the "mutually and equally profitable" agreements would not result in "injury or hurt to our own country," and that each agreement would reflect "care and caution by fully competent Government agencies."

Unlike earlier tariff legislation, the Trade Agreements Act was entirely an "enabling act," authorizing continual executive modification of American commercial relations. With the intermittent concluding of agreements, the public was periodically reminded of the policy. It obviously behooved the administration to develop and solidify popular support for the Program, which required extending legislation every few years.

Even before passage of the act, and continuing throughout the 1930's, State Department officials were concerned with the problem of maintaining congressional and public support. Hull's record is sufficient evidence of his sincerity and earnestness in advocating the reciprocity policy, and there is no reason to doubt the similar convictions of his subordinates. Continuation of the Program, however, depended largely on so analyzing the agreements that the effects of the policy would be construed as beneficial.

The Reasons for Trade. In Hull's view, as stated in the 1930's, the economic justification for trade stemmed from the uneven global distribution of natural resources. Countries specialized on production appropriate for their respective endowments of materials and exchanged their surpluses. Some nations depended on trade for their existence, and even the United States, potentially the most nearly self-sufficient country, would suffer a serious fall in productive efficiency and thus in her standard of living by trying to supply domestically all her needs. By importing, a nation drew upon resources and skills of the rest of the world, and by supplying its own exchange enabled others to buy its surpluses. Hull persisted in speaking of the pattern of specialization and of the gains from trade in terms of absolute, not comparative, costs.

There were, moreover, noneconomic advantages from trade. It spread knowledge of inventions and of science; it intermingled cultures and contributed to the general progress of civilization; and it was a great influence in the maintenance of peace.

Trade as the Basis of Prosperity. For Hull, the overriding economic reason for a liberal commercial policy was the essential contribution of trade to prosperity. With failure of the Paris Peace Conference after the First World War to promote a genuine economic restoration, and then with a perverted leadership toward isolation by the United States, most countries gravitated toward policies of autarky. Ever-narrowing trade practices—embracing many ingenious barriers and methods of discrimination, and climaxed by the American tariff of 1930—were largely responsible, in Hull's view, for the sharp decline of world commerce and thus even for the global depression.

The role of trade was to solve the "surplus" problem. "Full, stable, and permanent recovery" required maximum production, but, with all major economies specializing in particular products, this inevitably resulted in surpluses. Consequently, "each nation has come to regard foreign markets as the natural outlets for its surplus output."

Hull made it clear that, whatever ancillary benefits might be derived from the Trade Agreements Program, it was basically and originally designed as a recovery measure. When the bill was before Congress in 1934, he declared that "the problems of international commerce are at the very core of this country's economic dilemma," and in urging extension of the act in 1940, he still thought that "we all agree it was an act to promote exports." The Program was begun for "the express purpose of expanding our exports. . . . I submit that it has done so."

International trade policies could not, by themselves, insure a sound and lasting recovery. But neither were domestic policies adequate, unless accompanied by a program to increase exports.

Hull had advanced the trade agreements proposal originally as emergency legislation, and he continued to claim all through the period under review that the emergency persisted, in spite of progress toward prosperity. The Program had to be considered, therefore, as only temporary, and not until the end of the depression would it be appropriate to consider "permanent, normal tariff policies."

Problems of Imports. Hull recognized that a nation wishing to export must also import: "over a substantial period of time the goods and services which others buy from us must be paid for by the goods and services we buy from them." Moreover, it was foolish to countenance "the shabby heresy" that imports necessarily must be hurtful and that trade (and trade agreements) cannot be mutually profitable.

Hull explained at length that foreign trade has always been basically "complementary and non-competitive." Most imports, especially goods not produced domestically, were not "directly or seriously" competitive; some supplemented domestic production which could not meet the entire demand at a reasonable price; others met special requirements of quality, type, price, off-season marketing; included also were matrials for domestic industry. Trade could expand on a complementary basis only by minimizing barriers, with each country concentrating on production in which it was most efficient. "The more we encourage our efficient industries to find foreign markets, the more the structure of our industry will be shifted toward those lines which will not feel the impact of foreign competition. It is the country that seeks to protect unnatural industries which is always faced with foreign competition."

Perhaps Hull felt that few people found these arguments wholly convincing. One may speculate that in his own mind they were partly rationalizations to excuse the necessary acceptance of a large volume of imports in order to export surpluses. At any rate, he agreed to the desirability of maintaining "reasonable or moderate tariffs" that would prevent "abnormal, unreasonable, or materially hurtful imports" to the detriment of "any well-established and reasonably efficient domestic industry." And, according to the Secretary, the trade agreements organization was completely successful in providing ample safeguards for American industry while cautiously granting limited concessions. "These duty restrictions," he claimed, "have not inflicted any injury on any group of producers." "We have reduced duties only in those cases in which, after a most careful examination of all relevant factors, it was found that existing duties were unnecessarily and unduly burdensome, and we have done so only in those cases in which other countries have agreed to accord better treatment to our exports in return. . . . We have reduced duties only to the extent to which . . . it was found that such adjustments would not be prejudicial to any established branch of production." These "moderate and adequately safeguarded" concessions had been sufficiently attractive to other nations for them to grant in return a large number of valuable benefits to our export trade.

Labor and Agriculture under Trade Agreements. The great majority of laborers, Hull claimed, either were not directly associated with foreign trade or were engaged in export industries. All laborers were injured as consumers by tariffs. Reducing imports not only indirectly injured export industries, but the decline in exports depressed the general domestic market for home industry and agriculture. High wages depended upon "industrial efficiency," and it was the exporting industries—not those sheltered by tariffs—which were the most efficient and which paid the highest wages.

Because farmers supposedly sell most of their produce at world prices and buy frequently in tariff-protected markets, "it hardly needs to be recited that as a general proposition agriculture stands to gain far more by a liberal commercial policy and to lose more by a high tariff than other elements of our population." The core of his discussion was the demonstration of the fallacy of the slogan, "the American market for the American farmer." "This slogan ignores the fact that the American farmer has today, and has always had, practically all the American market for everything that could be produced in this country at reasonable cost. The domestic market simply is not big enough to absorb all of his production. In addition, he needs foreign markets."

As demonstrated by experience under the tariff of 1930, Hull claimed, embargo protection could result only in grave injury to export trade, both because of the nature of the mechanics of trade and because of foreign retaliation. And, as noted in the case of labor interests, curtailment of any portion of the general export trade would impair the capacity of the home market to absorb domestic production. Only rarely and with little emphasis did Hull consider the possibility of resource-shifting to correct a "surplus" problem. The condition of overextension of agriculture, due largely to war, was accepted as permanent, and the only solution was an expanded export trade.

With agriculture, as with domestic producers generally, the effects of the Program had been wholly beneficial: "no portion of agriculture has been materially injured even for the time being, even from the short-sighted view." There had been much agitation about "selling the farmer down the river," and a large part of Hull's explanation of the "complementary and non-competitive" nature of imports and his statistical analyses of the stimulation to exports was intended to mollify the farm interests.

Autarky, Equality, and United States Leadership. Hull spoke often and effectively about the disadvantages and dangers in the growth of autarky and of discrimination. Granting government trade advantages to one segment of the economy made inevitable granting such aid to every group; and after one nation embarked upon a program of controlled trade, other nations were almost certain to retaliate. Widespread policies of bilateral balancing quotas, exchange controls, "exaggerated protectionism," embargoes, and barter arrangements meant the disruption of the international price system and the consequent diversion of trade into unnatural channels, "a violent structural shift in international division of labor," the reduction of the total volume of trade, and the impossibility of normal and mutually profitable trade making its full contribution to general confidence, living standards, and economic and political stability. In addition, efficient political control of foreign trade would make necessary a high degree of regimentation in the domestic economy.

Hull declared that "our trade-agreements program has proven to be an instrument of policy more than able to hold its own in world markets against the most aggressive trade policies yet devised." He reasonably regarded as "a chief feature" of the Program—indeed, "the corner stone of American commercial policy"—the unconditional most-favored-nation principle. A policy granting exclusive concessions would necessarily involve discriminations, constant renegotiations, and uncertainty. The unconditional most-favored-nation clause, on the other hand, was to replace special bargaining and preferential arrangements with equality of treatment. The objection to which Hull replied again and again was that generalizing concessions meant "giving something for nothing." He emphasized that in fact this country did receive *quid pro quo:* our exports were protected against discrimination in foreign markets. Conversely, to receive the equal treatment which the

United States had always demanded, we had to extend it. Indeed, we gained more than an equal bargain, Hull claimed, for the value of our protected exports exceeded the value of our imports affected by generalized concessions.

The wave of economic nationalism after 1918, particularly with the beginning of the depression, was largely a result of United States policy, according to Hull. At the end of the war we ignored both the fact that the world required a rejuvenated trade as a basis for recovery and peace and the fact that the United States—now a creditor, unravaged by war and possessing extraordinary efficiency, having the good will of most of the world and a great demand for its produce—was in an unprecedented position to influence world economic development. But, with an "irrational fear of foreign competition," we pursued a policy of restricted trade which inspired and forced retaliation by others. For a time additional American loans moved surpluses, but Hull identified trade barriers as the major cause of the world economic collapse—which in turn led to still greater barriers.

The Great Depression did not deprive the United States of its economic pre-eminence, and Hull urged his country "to exert a determined leadership in the direction of liberal commercial policies." "We are willing frankly to admit that we have erred in the past, that we have now repented and wish to do works meet for repentance." The Trade Agreements Program announced our intention to assume liberal leadership, and he claimed it was eminently successful in achieving effective international co-operation in the interests of both prosperity and peace. Economic nationalism continued, but Hull insisted that there was no acceptable alternative to the ideals of the Program for those wishing to promote peace, economic welfare, and free enterprise. The outbreak of the Second World War should not cause an abandonment of the policy, although possibilities for expanding it would be limited. Not only to protect our immediate export trade, but to maintain the principles of liberal trade and to lay the ground work for postwar reorganization, the Program had to be continued.

International Trade and Peace. When the Program started, its basic purpose was to round out the recovery program.
Within a year or two Hull was fervently emphasizing its role
as a preserver of peace. He denied in the late 1930's that the
Program was at variance with its original intent of expanding
exports. But he left no doubt that the government "has enlarged the scope of its effort" to include "the broad, twin
objective of economic well-being and peace." "Prosperity and
peace go hand in hand. To promote one is to promote the
other." "The promotion of peace" was "the primary objective of our foreign policy," and the contribution which the
Program would make to this end was an "even more profound
reason" for restoring foreign commerce than the "purely economic" benefits that would obtain. "It is . . . the only comprehensive and basic program being pressed today which lays
a foundation for peace."

Economic considerations were crucial in analyzing political
and social problems: "economic barriers lie at the root of the
world's major ills." Hull offered a number of summaries of
the "principles which are essential to peace." He stressed
"adherence to the basic principles of justice, morality, good-
will, and friendliness which . . . underlie order under law";
but invariably and conspicuously he referred to the economic
conditions and policies "indispensable to a satisfactory international order."

Sometimes Hull did little more than assert that political,
military, and social developments have a governing economic
base, of which international trade is the controlling element.
"Economic stability, financial stability, social stability, and in
the last analysis political stability, are all parts of an arch
resting upon the foundation of trade."

His meager elaboration of this thesis contained three points.
First, general economic distress is inevitable to some extent in
the absence of flourishing commerce, and such distress "quickly
translates itself into social instability and political unrest";
nations finding themselves "hopelessly mired in economic
poverty and widespread privation" are relatively easy prey

for demagogues with chauvinistic schemes of aggression; and lack of normal access to foreign markets and materials causes international dissension and strongly inclines peoples to think in terms of military aggrandizement. In short, "there is no more dangerous cause of war than economic distress, and no more potent factor in creating such distress than stagnation and paralysis in the field of international commerce."

Second, nations will strive inexorably for "economic betterment"; it is imperative that they not be "misled into threatening to wrest from others by force of arms what [they] could have obtained much more satisfactorily by peaceful means"; stifling "normal economic processes" diminishes both freedom and economic welfare; international commerce is the prime means for peaceful advance and mutual gain. Increased trade would enhance aggregate productivity and also, by reducing tensions and animosities and replacing despair with hope, promote the shifting of resources out of armament industries.

Finally, the manner and spirit, as well as the volume, of trade is crucial: "fierce and unregulated struggles" for trade and frictions from illiberal trade practices tend to inspire enmity, mistrust, retaliation, and even overt military conflict. We "cannot assume that each growth in trade, no matter how attained means a growth in the promise of peace." "If nations are engaged in discrimination or retaliation or in the practice of irritating trade methods toward one another, the preservation of friendly relations and of that understanding necessary for peace and mutual prosperity is rendered difficult and precarious."

Typically, in discussing the relationships between economic circumstances and war, Hull pressed his argument in extreme terms. The primary reason why peoples may be incited to war is "their lack of a chance to produce and distribute and earn a living"; militarism develops "when people do not have enough to eat and to wear, nor anything to work with, and are idle." Only occasionally did he concede that "the matter of war and peace is [not] decided by economic developments alone" and deny "the claim that the trade-agreements program is an immediate guarantee of peace regardless of all else."

III

In many of its provisions, in most of its administrative procedures, and to a considerable degree in its underlying philosophy, the Reciprocal Trade Agreements Program represents a major innovation in American tariff history. Moreover, in 1934, when the act was signed, the Program was a unique national policy in the world economic community and represented to many, in the later observation of Sumner Welles, "one spark of sanity in a world outlook that seemed wholly and hopelessly dark."

The remaining dislocations of the First World War had been compounded by the effects of the great global depression. With severe employment and national income difficulties throughout the world, international trade was typically conceived as a tool of economic nationalism rather than as a means of increasing real incomes through international specialization and subsequent multilateral exchange. The Trade Agreements Program was begun in a most inauspicious period. But it remained the core of United States commercial policy until the Second World War, and since the war it has been renewed periodically and expanded in the General Agreement on Tariffs and Trade.

It must be conceded, however, that Hull's arguments in support of the Program are studded with deficiencies in theory. With reference to a fundamental matter, while he realized that there are gains to be derived from foreign trade and that somehow the basis of trade is associated with the pattern of global resource endowment, he described the gains from trade as stemming from the exportation of "surplus production." In discussing the problem of employment, he held that "losses and dislocations resulting from shrunken foreign trade cannot possibly be compensated by mere increase of domestic trade." It is true that, given international specialization and a system of interchanging "surpluses," a decline in the export markets of a country will create difficulties for it. But, assuming that resources in the export industries have some mobility, the long-run problems will be essentially those of optimum allocation of resources, not those of the full employment of resources. Like most participants in public tariff debates, Hull failed to make clear that the basic purpose of international trade is not to act as a lever for raising the level of economic activity—now, at least, there are better tools for this task—but rather to promote efficiency in allocating the world's resources. A permanent reduction of trade may well result in a permanent reduction of real incomes from what they otherwise would have been, but it does not imply a permanent reduction of employment.

Hull, however, seemed implicitly to deny a critical assumption, viz., the mobility of resources now in export industries. Thus if exports decline, these permanently committed factors must face unemployment. What of the mobility of resources in industries competing with imports? Hull chose, probably wisely on tactical grounds, not to face this related problem squarely and consistently. At times he spoke as if this were scarcely a problem: typically, imports are "complementary and non-competitive." At other places he made references to productive specialization on the basis of efficiency and the ability to meet foreign competition, with the implication that inefficient producers, "unnatural industries," should drop by the wayside. But most clearly enunciated were the assurances that United States concessions, moderate and cautiously granted, had not, and never would, injure "any well-established and reasonably efficient industry."

Increased exports were considered a result of trade agreement concessions obtained; increased imports were imputed to other factors, notably droughts. This was spectacular diplomacy, indeed: a great deal supposedly was obtained at virtually no "cost." But economic theory—in light of developing balance of payments disequilibria over the world, the American post-First World War creditor position, and the welfare aspects of increasing imports and of promoting international specializa-

tion on the basis of comparative advantage—gives little cause
for enthusiasm for the *objective* of greatly expanding exports
while preventing harm to any domestic industry from enlarged
imports.

Hull was much more concerned with the level of aggregate
employment than with the efficiency of employment. And
since the United States accumulated "surpluses" and experienced
a reduction of exports while the depression deepened, he concluded that the depression was due primarily to the decline in
trade. No doubt the causal relationship ran both ways—exports are a determinant of national income and imports are a
disposition of income—but it was rarely suggested that the
level of trade was a partial function of the level of economic
activity.

Hull was not content to defend the Program on the restricted grounds of commercial benefits. It was also a major
aspect of the policy to promote peace.

There is an element of plausibility in Hull's sweeping dicta
pertaining to economic forces and conditions as the motivating
influence in most political and social activity. However, few
economists would make these claims to the same degree and
with the same assurance. It is easier to accept Hull's conclusions that there may be, and indeed frequently have been,
"economic causes" of international conflict and war and that
commonly followed policies of substantially free trade probably will contribute to the maintenance of peace. But Hull
sometimes couched his assertions in simple, quasi-emotional
terms, in terms of inducing people and nations to do "right"
instead of "wrong." The civilizing qualities of foreign trade,
if any, are surely to be applauded and encouraged, but probably
few today put much reliance on trade's bringing out the "goodness" of people. It is not certain even that there is a high
positive correlation between "prosperity and peace," as Hull
claimed; indeed, some have suggested that such correlation as
there may be is negative. Hull would seem to have been on
firmer ground in decrying those unilateral, arbitrary, unpre-
dictable, and discriminatory trade policies which inevitably in-

duced doubts, fears, and antagonisms among the world economic community.

Perhaps as big a deficiency as any in Hull's thought in this area was his failure to indicate clearly the probable reciprocal relationship between the maintenance of peace and reasonably free trade. We have noted his view of an one-way causal association between trade and national income, when in fact they are interrelated. Similarly, it can be convincingly argued that peace is as much a condition for a system of substantially free trade, as that freedom of trade is a necessary condition of peace. But Hull stressed only the latter relationship.

Despite the inelegance of the Secretary's presentations, they were characterized by a coherence, breadth of view, and sophistication which placed them on a level considerably higher than that of typical congressional tariff debates. Moreover, while it is legitimate and useful to apply criteria of theory in analyzing debates on public policy, in the long run neither the goodness of intentions of policy-makers nor the degree of academic comprehension of issues is in itself the crucial matter, but rather the actual consequences of operations in the market place. Other things the same, presumably the better the intentions and the greater the comprehension, the more satisfactory will be public policy, but in fact policy inevitably is a resultant of many factors in addition to the philosophies and theories of public officials. In particular, a reasonable judgment of policy and policy proposals should not be made alone in clear-cut "absolute" terms deduced from abstract analysis but also in relative terms with respect to possible alternative policies.

We may grant that (*a*) Hull was deficient in much of his analysis, (*b*) the Trade Agreements Program was not wholly adequate either as a commercial policy or as a preventer of war, and (*c*) perhaps the basic assumptions and presumptions on which the Program was based were too idealistic, too purely a carry-over from the nineteenth century. Still, in our evaluation of Hull and the Program, we should do well to keep in mind the nature of United States tariff history, the complex problems and the volatile circumstances of the time, and the feasible alternatives which may have been available. If the United States had not taken the lead toward a degree of international economic co-operation, would any other nation have done so? If Hull had not pressed a policy of commercial liberalism for the United States, would anyone else have done so? If Hull had proposed and defended the Trade Agreements Program on strictly "economists' " grounds, how would he have fared? If he had failed to get either the Program or a better alternative, would the United States have accomplished so much in the past twenty-odd years (little though it may be) or have so satisfactory a commercial policy now (poor and uncertain though it may be)?

In the final acounting, few economists would deny that, both as an actual, operating program and as a symbol of American ideals and an indication of American criteria of appropriate policy, the Trade Agreements Program is an asset. It surely is not the best that we could have hoped for, but it probably comes close to being the best that we could reasonably have expected.

6. *William L. Neumann*

Ambiguity and Ambivalence in Ideas of National Interest in Asia

Foreign policies, like commodities, carry price tags. There are few bargains and no giveaways. Nations achieve what they are willing to pay for and no more.

SAMUEL L. SHARP

AMBIGUITY rather than clarity, ambivalence rather than consistency and singleness of purpose have been characteristic of American thought about the role of the United States in Asia. In the early decades of this century many Americans held that there were no important national interests in the Far East. More recently there has been some agreement about the existence of national interests in this area without consensus as to their nature. Means as well as ends are involved in the argument. The crux of the debate has often been the question of what policies would and what policies would not achieve the desired objectives. The debaters' differences have been frequently reducible to disparities in their estimates of the cost and returns of a particular policy. Proponents of a policy tend to see the price set at a bargain low while opponents view it as prohibitively high.

Estimating the limits of national power, some have concluded that no policy could, under existing conditions, achieve a desired goal in Asia. Objectives which require policies involving manpower, wealth, and morale beyond a nation's willingness or ability to provide can be catastrophic. Facing the turbulence of modern China, Secretary of State Dean Acheson decided that in some respects nothing could be done "until the dust settles." General Douglas MacArthur recognized American limitations when he told Congress in 1951 that "no man in his right mind would advocate sending our ground forces into continental China." A policy which would require American conquest and control of over six hundred million Chinese might pose a threat to national survival rather than serving national interests.

Given the limits of national power, it is always incumbent upon the makers of American policy to establish priorities of national interests. Some interests are obviously more vital than others and of greater concern to the nation as a whole. The uncontrolled pursuance of one interest may at times obstruct the advancement of another. When the most basic interest of Americans has been peace the maintenance or advancement of the other interests by policies involving the threat of force has been handicapped. In more recent decades, when "security" seems to have replaced "peace" as the word describing the most important national interest, other interests have been sacrificed to this concept.

A system of priority of national interests requires some consistency and clarity of definition. Yet a concept like security defies an objective definition. What constitutes security, how much is essential, and by what means it can be achieved— these questions cannot be answered with any universality or finality. Applied to the Far East, the concept of security has been invoked by those who said it required a program of American withdrawal, and by those who said it called for more active involvement.

The definition of national interests, even in a democracy, remains in most instances the task of a tiny minority. Prior to the Second World War areas like the Far East were remote from the experience of most Americans, and bona fide expressions of public opinion about American interests in Asia were rare. A few score Far Eastern experts and foreign policy specialists covered current events with books and articles and often urged particular policies. The Institute of Pacific Relations, the Foreign Policy Association, and a few organizations with economic, religious, or cultural interests in Asia also appealed to the public and to government in behalf of particular objectives. The influence of these groups was not limited by the size of their constituency since on some occasions it was enough to have the ear of the President, Secretary of State, or some other highly placed government official.

I

By 1920 the Far East had become a vigorous rival of Europe as an area of major diplomatic importance for the United States. The main body of American naval power was moved from the Atlantic to the North Pacific in 1919, and except for cruising exercises the concentration of naval strength remained in the Pacific for the next two decades. In the early twenties over a quarter of the State Department's overseas diplomatic personnel was assigned to Far Eastern posts, and the staffs of the embassies at Peking and Tokyo were larger than those at London and Paris. Far Eastern questions had assumed great importance in the Senate debates over approval of the Paris Peace Treaty in 1919 and 1920. Writers who looked gloomily into the future and saw another war consistently located its genesis in the Pacific.

China was assigned the largest American diplomatic delegation and was first in importance in the Far East. A chief of the Far Eastern Division of the State Department, John V. A. MacMurray, concluded: ". . . our government policy as well as popular opinion put China at the center of its thinking on Far Eastern affairs—made it the sun to which Japan and even our own Philippine possessions were merely planetary." Since the first American contacts with Asia, China had claimed this pre-eminence. The earliest transpacific trade had centered on China, and it was in China that the first American commercial interests were established. American religious and philanthropic groups gave the Chinese the greatest attention. The cornerstone of American Far Eastern policy, the Open Door concept, had its origins in relations with China.

Many Americans interested in Far Eastern trade considered China to be the most important Asian market. These considerations were based on future prospects rather than present accomplishments, and since the 1890's China had been acclaimed as providing America with a New World as the Western Hemisphere had done for England, France, and Spain. Four hundred million customers with primitive wants, untouched by the magic wand of modern advertising—this was a tantalizing field for an industrial and commercial nation. By 1920 there was evidence that this market could expand under proper encouragement. Cigarette sales, for example, had grown from approximately one cigarette a year for each Chinese in 1900 to nineteen a year in 1920. If every adult Chinese could be encouraged to consume even one smoke daily, American tobacco producers and exporters would enjoy a golden future.

Economic interest in China commonly ignored Japan and typified the pro-Chinese bias which put more emphasis on hopes than realities. By the turn of the century Japanese trade with the United States already exceeded that with China, and by 1920 the value of American sales to Japan was almost five times that of sales to China. Japanese industrialization and the rising standard of living, for which China would have to wait many decades, more than offset Japan's inferiority in numbers of customers. The China market never did boom as expected. In 1950 an American Secretary of State warned a Communist Chinese government that China's market for American goods was so insignificant that it could not be used to extort concessions from the United States.

American interest in China and the Far East, according to some official statements, is not an economic one. Our concern for the Far East, said Cordell Hull, is "not measured by the number of American citizens residing in a particular country at a particular moment nor by the amount of investment of American citizens there nor by the volume of trade." According to Henry L. Stimson, our interest in China is rooted in "our political and humanitarian idealism." A third Secretary of State, Dean Acheson, broadened the concept and said that American interest in the peoples of Asia is in people alone: "We do not want to use them for any purpose of our own."

Measured by the humanitarian activities of Americans in the Orient, the noneconomic interests have been important.

The first American missionary began the task of trying to convert the Chinese to Christianity in 1829. By 1920 over three thousand Americans were working in Chinese missions, schools, and hospitals, and the total capital investment in this work was over twelve million dollars. Japan ranked a poor second with only a thousand missionaries and an investment of some two million. Although a century of American effort in China combined with European efforts to win converts totaling less than one-tenth of 1 per cent of the Chinese population, individual conversions have had great significance. The most influential achievement was the confession of faith made by Chiang Kai-shek at the behest of the Southern Methodist Church. The role of another Christianized family, the Soongs, has also been important in Chinese-American relations.

Chinese missionaries have been the most influential of all groups interested in American Far Eastern policy. Churches all over the United States have supported one or more workers in China, and, as Henry L. Stimson explained:

The news of the work of these missionaries coming through their reports and letters reached a large number of our people living in almost every quarter of the land. To many of them the progress of this work was one of their keenest interests. They . . . acquired a humanitarian interest of a quite personal character in that land and its people.

The relations of the missionaries with American diplomatic officials were close, and information obtained from missionaries often influenced reports sent to Washington. On returning home missionaries often visited the State Department to report and confer with interested officials.

Missionaries and missionary children have influenced American policy and opinion in other ways. The Chief of the Far Eastern Division of the State Department during the crucial years 1914-1918 and adviser on Far Eastern problems at Paris in 1919 was E. T. Williams, a former Chinese missionary. Walter Judd spent more than a decade as a medical

missionary in China before returning to the United States in
1938 and entering Congress as an authority on Chinese questions and a faithful defender of the Kuomintang. A missionary's
son, Henry R. Luce, was born in China and maintained an
interest and point of view about China which entered millions
of American homes through the Luce publications. A daughter
of a missionary, Pearl Buck, taught in China for a decade and
in 1931 published *The Good Earth,* a best-selling book which
left hundreds of thousands of readers with a warmly sympathetic stereotype of the Chinese peasant. The Japanese
farmer has never been as fortunate in inspiring literary expressions in the United States. The favorable climate of opinion within which Americans viewed China prior to the
Korean War in 1950 owes much to the missionary movement.

Japan in 1920 was at the opposite pole of American Far
Eastern policy. Japanese-American relations had a background of friendship and benevolence going back to the days
of Commodore Matthew Perry's penetration of Japanese isolation. Americans were concerned that Japan avoid China's
fate at the hands of the European imperialists, and officially
as well as unofficially the United States helped Japan to build
its naval, military, and industrial strength. But when Japan
in 1895 administered a surprising defeat to China, far-sighted
Americans began to whisper that Japan might be a future rival
in the Pacific. After Japan's defeat of Russia in 1905 these
whispers rose to a shout. The American image of Japan was
transformed in a few decades from that of a grateful pupil
of Westernization; Japan was seen instead as an ambitious
upstart, a Yellow Peril, threatening the white man's supremacy
in Asia.

The First World War and Japan's issuance of the Twenty-
One Demands on China in 1915 accelerated the change in
the American image. Woodrow Wilson in February of 1917
told his cabinet that if a do-nothing policy in regard to the
European war would "keep the white race or part of it strong
to meet the Yellow Race—Japan, for instance, in alliance with
Russia [from] dominating China," he was willing to put

European issues aside. The stop-Japan advocates were strong in American councils at the Paris Peace Conference, and Wilson agreed to the unpleasant business of sending an American military expedition into Siberia to counter Japan's forces.

Japan, like China, had its sympathetic Americans, although few in number. The Japan Society, founded in New York in 1907, included influential business and financial leaders like August Belmont and Jacob Schiff. By 1913 the Society had grown to a thousand members and worked energetically that year to counter a Japanese war scare. In addition to economic interests in the friendship of Japan, American missionaries set forth the case for good relations in articles, books, and pamphlets. The limits of the strength of these groups was demonstrated in 1924, however, when their protests failed to move Congress to drop the Japanese Exclusion section from the new immigration legislation.

Japanese interest groups had not only to compete with pro-Chinese groups, but also with the racialism of the West Coast which in the twentieth century turned from Chinese to the Japanese threat. Racialism entered Japanese-American relations with the San Francisco school case in 1906; it played a part in Wilson's rejection of the principle of equal treatment of all peoples in the League of Nations Covenant, and reached a high with the abrogation of the Gentlemen's Agreement about Japanese immigration in 1924.

The third major area of American interest in Asia in 1920 was in the Philippines. Here the importance of economic, idealistic, and other interests was subordinate to the impact of American possession on relations with Japan. Nine years after the American flag was first raised over Manila, Theodore Roosevelt concluded that these islands were "our heel of Achilles" and "all that makes the present situation with Japan dangerous." The hope that the Philippines would be a stepping stone to the trade of Asia soon dissolved. By the time of American entry into the First World War, Secretary of State Robert Lansing was wishing that it were possible to save American "face" and still dispose of the islands to Japan.

Korea, which thirty years later was to become a fourth Far Eastern area of important American interests, was not in 1920 an area of concern. Both Theodore Roosevelt and William Howard Taft had acquiesced in the expansion of Japanese interests in Korea which led to annexation in 1910. Few Americans had any knowledge of Korea a decade later. Korean nationalists, led by Syngman Rhee, had tried to enlist American support for their nation's independence at the end of the First World War, and stories were told of Korean villages looking to the skies for airplanes which would bring Woodrow Wilson and independence. But Korean nationalism had not yet touched the American impulse to liberate.

II

At no time in the interwar period did any responsible government official make a public and explicit statement of the priorities of American interest in Asia. The relationship of these interests to American interests in other areas remained ambiguous, and which interests in Asia, if any, were vital enough to justify war in their behalf was never clarified. Perhaps the historian is asking for the impossible in seeking such a clarification in a democratic state where any statement of priorities of interests has obvious political complications. But, to be effective, policy must be guided by some principles in a world of finite power and resources. No one of the three Republican administrations nor the one Democratic administration in the period between the two World Wars seems to have reached agreement on a consistent system of priorities. The historian can do little more than draw some conclusions about this system from government action in a number of specific situations.

Two major problems faced the American policy-makers in this period. The first was the protection of American citizens and their property from depredations by the Chinese. The second was the protection of American citizens, property, and China itself from the ravages of Japanese expansionism.

The first problem was dominant in the nineteen twenties and the second in the thirties.

At the roots of both problems were some of the same basic conditions: the rise of Chinese nationalism, with its antiforeign manifestations, and the political instability which invited foreign intervention. Chinese nationalism, which had given warning of its future with the Boxer Rebellion in 1900, was intensified in the twentieth century. The spread of modern education, helped by foreign mission schools and colleges, produced successive generations of young Chinese whose first political objective was the expulsion of the occidental intruders. Japan demonstrated the vulnerability of the white man by defeating Russia in 1905 and by driving the Germans out of China and the Pacific during the First World War. Following the close of the Washington Conference in 1922, Chinese nationalists launched a sustained effort to end the treaty rights of the Western nations in China itself.

Unlike European nationalism in the nineteenth century, Chinese nationalism did not lead directly to the establishment or strengthening of a central government. From the republican revolution of 1911 onward China at no time had a dynamic national government which exercised effective control over all the area to which it claimed sovereignty. Until the triumph of the Communist forces in 1949, power was decentralized. Many areas were in the control of military governors whose troops were loyal only to their commander. The governors themselves were in many instances no more than war lords whose chief interest was the plundering of the area under their control. While Peking remained the nominal capital to which American ministers were accredited in the twenties, the rule of the Peking government at times barely extended beyond the city walls.

American policy-makers were faced with large-scale destruction of property and the killing and kidnaping of American citizens. The Chinese government appeared helpless to forestall such events, and only under strong diplomatic pressure did it act to punish the offenders and pay indemnities.

Chinese opinion expressed disdain for the treaty structure which guided relations with foreign powers and which was reaffirmed at the Washington Conference in 1921-1922. Despite China's protests the United States and the European powers were agreed that China must put its house in order as a prerequisite to the modification or termination of extraterritorial rights. Two years after the close of the Washington Conference, China demanded the speedy end of extraterritoriality; the foreign powers argued in reply that conditions were so turbulent that foreign residents and interests were in even greater need of special protection.

There were three theoretical policies open to the United States vis-a-vis rising Chinese antiforeignism: complete withdrawal, partial withdrawal and limited use of force, or unlimited military action to restore order and to uphold treaty rights. If American interests were judged important enough to justify the cost in lives and resources, an effort could have been made at military occupation, alone or in collaboration with other foreign powers. The end would have been the establishment of order and of a regime favorable to foreign interests and the treaty system. This was one of Japan's unilateral goals beginning with war on Manchuria in 1931 and on Northern China begining in 1937. Judging by the resistance Japan met, serious doubts must be raised about the success of a policy even a decade earlier. The effort to pacify an area as extensive as China would have strained American manpower and morale. If success was possible, it could have been achieved only after years of warfare. The maintenance of a pro-American regime in the face of growing Chinese nationalism would have been a constant drain on the power of the United States and on any possible allies.

In the public mind and in Congress as well peace or no-war probably was the major national interest in the 1920's. Any view of the Far East consistent with this major interest had to down-grade regional interests accordingly. The House Military Affairs Committee in 1922 reported out the Army Appropriation Bill with a proviso that no money could be used to pay troops stationed in China unless there was a declared "state of emergency." Although defeated on the floor, this effort to limit the use of force in Asia reflected widespread opinion. Secretary of State Charles Evans Hughes wrote the Secretary of War in 1922 that it was not a part of this nation's purpose "to impress upon the Chinese government or people the military power or prestige of this country." Two years later Hughes told a group of American businessmen with interests in China that, short of a threatened disaster like the Boxer Rebellion, "the state of domestic opinion in this country would not permit the dispatch of any further considerable military forces to China."

Two practical policies remained. One was to recognize that the day of the white man was rapidly drawing to an end in Asia, to liquidate interests as rapidly as possible, and to proclaim the area "out of bounds" for American businessmen, missionaries, and tourists while the antiforeign spirit was uncontrolled. Such a policy called for drastic action, but it merited serious official consideration as late as 1937. When President Roosevelt in that year warned Americans to leave China, Secretary of Interior Harold Ickes told the other members of the cabinet, "We oughtn't to be expected to go to war, with all the dreadful consequences involved, to protect people who are doing something they want to do"; therefore those Americans who remained in China should have no claim to government protection. Although Secretary Hughes seems to have inclined towards complete withdrawal in the early twenties, he never dared face the ire of the missionary and business groups as well as the ultra-nationalists who believed that an American had a right to full protection wherever he went.

The other policy—that actually followed by Hughes, Frank Kellogg, and Henry Stimson until 1931—was to accept the limits of armed intervention in China and to use force only in coastal cities where a substantial number of American residents were in immediate danger. In September, 1924, Secretary Hughes authorized the dispatch of eleven naval vessels to

Shanghai and the landing of marines when civil war raged in that area. By 1928 there were as many as 3,000 marines concentrated at Tientsin and 1,000 at Shanghai. But if the Chinese had forced a showdown, it is unlikely that any administration would have risked the political repercussions of sizable American casualties in China, even if justified as "police action." American naval vessels of the Yangtze patrol were attacked thirty-seven times within a few months in 1927 by Chinese troops, but the State Department went no further than protests.

Despite this realistic adjustment of policy to the current definition of national interests, there were other elements in American thought about Asia which created future difficulties. The most significant of these was the persistence of a benevolent image of China which produced ambivalent attitudes towards the nationalist movement. The benevolent image plus the tradition of American anti-imperialism led to the assumption that the nationalist movement was not only a commendable expression of the desire for self-determination, but would favor American national interests as well. Secretary of State Frank Kellogg frequently stated his belief that the triumph of the nationalist movement and the abolition of extraterritoriality would improve Chinese-American relations. President Coolidge in April, 1927, stated his faith that "ultimately" the turmoil in China would end and that "some form of authority will emerge which will no doubt be prepared to make adequate settlement for any wrongs we have suffered." A competent Far Eastern expert, G. Nye Steiger, wrote in 1925, "the only possible course" for the United States to follow was "graceful submission to the national aspirations of the Chinese people." In his advice Steiger may have been right, but he went on to say that "there appears little reason to fear that the triumph of nationalism will endanger the legitimate aspirations of western commerce and investment."

This disregard for the price which *all* Western nations would ultimately pay for the triumph of Oriental nationalism expressed a faith in American destiny in Asia. European interests were "imperialistic," but American interests were basically humanitarian and concerned primarily with China's welfare. Such a distinction may have some validity, but the benevolence of the American interests did not produce any deep or lasting differentiation in the Chinese mind. A movement to "expel the foreign barbarians," irrational in its extreme nationalism, did not in practice make a radical distinction between those white men who claimed to be anti-imperialist and those whose interests were blatant economic exploitation. The administrations of Presidents Coolidge and Hoover went on record as favoring the success of Chinese nationalism. The United States refused to join other treaty powers in any sustained effort to hold the line against the antiforeign spirit and to insist on full compliance with treaty rights. Yet American negotiations with China for the termination of the "unequal treaties" broke down when neither Secretary Kellogg nor Secretary Stimson was willing to go unambiguously the whole way and to leave Americans and American interests to the mercies of Chinese law and Chinese courts. Viewed in retrospect, there appears to have been no half-way point between acquiescence and resistance to the nationalist spirit which promised to advance American interests.

III

In 1931 Japan turned to the use of force to protect its interests in Manchuria against a nationalist war lord. According to John MacMurray, Chief of the State Department's Far Eastern Division from 1919 to 1924, the Japanese government had been "in the belief of the diplomatic representatives of all countries in China at the time, scrupulously loyal in its adherence to the letter and spirit of the Washington Conference." Scrupulousness and tolerance of disorder were discarded in September, 1931, when the Japanese militarists began a campaign which ended in not only conquering Manchuria, but in trying to conquer all of northern China as well. By any quantitative measurement, Japan's interests in Manchuria and North China far exceeded that of other foreign nations. Many Japanese believed that the economic development of these areas was a vital national interest, essential not only to Japan's economic well-being, but to Japanese security by blocking further extension into Asia of Russian power. For this national interest Japan went to war against China and eventually against the United States as well.

In the world of nations, each side, in Herbert Butterfield's phrase, becomes "locked in its own system of self-righteousness," and the obstacles to the understanding of another nation's vital interests become almost insurmountable. Americans were very ambiguous about their own national interests in Asia; to understand Japan's interests was beyond the ability of most policy-makers. Any understanding was further blocked by the fact that Japan had broken the peace and had launched a full-scale war. The tradition of benevolence towards China, the background of suspicion of Japan, the sympathy of Americans for the "underdog"—all combined to label the Chinese cause "just" while the Japanese argument was dismissed *in toto* as the propaganda of an "aggressor."

The frustrations produced in pro-Chinese Americans by the excesses of Chinese nationalism were relieved by having a specific devil against which to direct their fire. A Japan at war against a weaker nation also provided a target for those racialist groups of Americans whose real enemy was the Japanese-American population of the West Coast. The triumph of these racialists came, not with Japan's surrender in 1945, but with the issuance of the Evacuation Order of February, 1942, summarily moving the Japanese and Japanese-American population into internment camps behind barbed wire and armed patrols.

Economics also contributed to the framework of bias with which Americans viewed the outbreak of war in Asia. When the American market for Japanese silk declined after 1929, Japanese exporters gave more attention to cheap consumer goods. A variety of items stamped "Made in Japan" appeared on American counters, and the alarmists cried out against the Japanese trade menace. When boycotts were organized against Japan because of the Sino-Japanese conflict, they found support in labor and manufacturing groups. Few Americans noted that Japan actually increased its purchases of American raw cotton during the depression years, that American chain stores were sending buyers to Japan to encourage production of cheap goods, and that the balance of trade favored the United States from 1932 onward. The American image of Japan comprised a racial menace, a threat to American interests in Asia, a disturber of world peace, and a trade menace as well.

The conquest of Manchuria and the subsequent extension of Japanese power into China itself led to a reconsideration of national interest in the thirties on the part of many Americans. One section of thought, dominant in the Roosevelt administration at least as late as 1937, gave American interests in China no greater priority than they had in the previous decade. Since war had not been justified to defend these interests against Chinese nationalism, its use was still not justified to defend the same interests against Japanese expansion. No great importance was given to the maintenance of the treaty structure per se, and the maintenance of the Kellogg-Briand Anti-War Pact no more required the use of war in its behalf than did the Washington treaties of 1922.

Secretary of State Hughes spoke for this point of view when he told American delegates to the Washington Conference that this country "would never go to war over any aggression on the part of Japan in China." Ten years later a former Secretary of State, Elihu Root, could still write that it had "never entered the head" of any American President or Secretary of State to send forces to China in defense of the Open Door. The Political Adviser to the Department of State, Stanley K. Hornbeck, concluded in 1936 that this country should "still proceed on the principle of playing no favorites" as between China and Japan and that there was "no intention of using force for the preservation of the 'open door.'" Nelson T. Johnson, Ambassador to China, wrote to Cordell Hull in January of the same year: "I do not want to be considered as one who believes that the American Government should bestir itself to use force to save China from probable Japanese conquest."

Even after the outbreak of the Sino-Japanese conflict in the summer of 1937 the State Department seems to have given less attention to the Far East than in the previous decade. Between 1922 and 1938 the size of the State Department's Foreign Service staff increased by 26 per cent, but only a few of these additional officers were sent to the Far East. Whereas over a quarter of the total Foreign Service served in the Far East in 1922, by 1938 this distribution had shrunk to almost 20 per cent. The embassy in Tokyo had only 16 men in 1938 compared to 26 in 1922 while the embassies in the two European centers of tension, Rome and Berlin, had increased their staffs. The Department's Far Eastern division had doubled its number of desk officers in the same period, but the same increases were made in the European divisions. The allocation of the resources of the State Department suggests a diminished rather than a greater importance assigned to Asia in the sixteen years after the Washington Conference.

Outside of government, competent students of American foreign policy also upheld the judgment that American interests in Asia were not worth a war. An eminent diplomatic historian, Samuel F. Bemis, praised Charles Evans Hughes in 1936 for having "the sanest conception" of American Far Eastern interests. Bemis urged that Americans follow Hughes's policy and remain "shocked but not involved bystanders to Japanese aggressions." One of the most prolific of popular writers about Far Eastern politics, Nathaniel Peffer, questioned in 1937 whether an American war against Japan would really help China. Former Secretary of State Stimson, once an advocate of sterner measures, raised the same query in a public letter in the fall of 1937, ". . . in my opinion this is not a case where there should be any thought of America sending armies to participate in a strife that is going on in Asia . . . to attempt it would do much more harm than good." Instead, Stimson placed his faith in the efficacy of a trade embargo against Japan.

A few astute students of world politics opposed war against Japan, not on grounds of the low priority of American interests in China, but because they viewed Japan as a necessary force to balance the historic ambitions of Russia in Asia. A leading American textbook on Far Eastern affairs, published in 1931, pointed out that Soviet policy was similar to Tsarist policy and that Russia was still aspiring to dominate Asia. "Russia is more to be feared by Japan and China than either of these is to be feared by the other," wrote Professors Hosea Morse and Harley MacNair in their *Far Eastern International Relations*. John MacMurray reinforced this conclusion in a State Department memorandum in 1935 when he pointed out that the defeat of Japan would "merely create a new set of stresses and substitute for Japan, the U. S. S. R. . . . as a contestant for the mastery of the East." MacMurray glimpsed the future and predicted, "If we were to 'save' China from Japan and become 'Number One' nation in the eyes of her people, we should thereby become not the most favored, but the most distrusted of nations." This type of evaluation of the historic role of Russia in Asia seems to have received little consideration in official American circles, not because of a widespread sympathy for Communism as is often charged, but because of a characteristic American naïveté and blindness when it came to recognizing the operational forces in world politics. Few recalled the insights of Theodore Roosevelt, who played off Japan against Russia in American interest. Many held to the belief that the Chinese, as a uniquely spiritual and tradition-bound people, would never accept the materialism of a Marxist, Western ideology.

A second section of American thought was made up of those who believed in doing something—or everything—short of war to stop Japanese expansion. Included in this group were many individuals who believed that the road to world peace was to be found in collective action in the form of moral pronouncements backed by "the weight of world opinion." This argument sought support in a misinterpretation of the influence of the Open Door pronouncement. As one congress-

man recalled this policy in the early twenties, Secretary of
State John Hay had "merely waved his hand" and thus saved
China from partition by European imperialists. Henry Stimson upheld the same almost mystical view of American influence in 1936; after describing conditions in nineteenth-
century China, he wrote, "John Hay checked that chaos."
The faith that words alone could change another nation's
definition of its national interests accounts for some of the
support given to the Stimson Non-recognition Doctrine of
1932. By refusing to accept the *de facto* status of Japan's
Manchukuo some strength was to be given to the treaty structure without bloodshed. Stimson himself later admitted that
the treaty system no more fitted the Asian situation than "a
stovepipe hat would fit an African savage," but he held to
the importance of taking some action in its behalf.

Stimson and many of the supporters of moral and legal
pronouncements against Japan were willing to go further and
support these verbal measures with economic sanctions and
even a show of force, if necessary. It was generally assumed
that Japan would buckle under economic pressures and draw
back from actual hostilities when faced by American power.
The intimidation of Japan by naval demonstrations had a tradition dating back to the Perry expedition, and within a limited
framework the bluff of force could claim numerous successes.
In 1932, at the request of the Department of State, American
fleet maneuvers at Hawaii were extended for two weeks to
emphasize American displeasure with Japanese expansion.
Stimson judged that this use of the Navy had "undoubtedly
exercised a steadying effect."

The last effort at naval intimidation and the most serious
in its consequences was made in 1940-1941. In April, 1940,
the fleet was moved from the West Coast to Hawaii for annual
maneuvers. The planned return to the coast in May was can-
celed by President Roosevelt personally since he believed the
advanced position of American naval power would have a
"deterrent effect" on Japanese aspirations to move into the
Dutch East Indies. The fleet commander, Admiral James O.

Richardson, was concerned about the vulnerability of his naval forces; bluffing on an international scale requires some consideration of the possibility of the bluff being called. But when Admiral Harold R. Stark, Chief of Naval Operations, took up the question with Richardson as to what would be done if Japan *did* go into the East Indies, he wrote, "My answer to that is, I don't know and I think there is nobody on God's green earth who can tell you." Richardson presented the case for the fleet's vulnerability to the President in person and was shortly after relieved of his command. The decision to use the fleet as a diplomatic weapon stood, and American naval forces were still at Pearl Harbor on the morning of December 7, 1941.

Americans who believed that Japanese expansion could be checked only by force and who favored using American force to this end constituted a tiny minority throughout the 1930's, even to the day of Pearl Harbor. Of those who held this position only a few dared brave the wrath of the strong antiwar sentiment by speaking out in favor of fighting. President Roosevelt discussed the subject of war with Japan with his peace-minded cabinet as early as March 7, 1933, but this discussion was more of an expression of his interest in naval strategy than of a willingness to act. In the fall of 1936 Mr. Roosevelt told his cabinet he was considering a further program of neutralization in the Pacific which would include the Alaskan territory nearest Japan and American Samoa. When Secretary of the Navy Claude Swanson called for war in September, 1937, two months after the renewal of war in China, the President told his cabinet that he was "a pacifist" and had no intention of making any warlike moves. The sinking of the *U.S.S. Panay* by Japanese planes in December, 1937, led Admiral William Leahy to urge that the fleet be prepared for action at sea, a move supported by the President's adviser, Norman H. Davis and Assistant Secretary of State, R. Walton Moore. But the President and other members of his staff resisted any provocative action.

The outbreak of the European war in September, 1939, and the fall of France in the summer of 1940 created new complications for American thought about the Far East. Hitler became the number one enemy for many Americans, and the European conflict demanded first priority. Those who favored the use of force to check aggression were torn between Europe and Asia. A Europe-first group of Americans recognized the tremendous burdens which a two-ocean war would impose. Consideration was now given to stalling for time in the Pacific and even to appeasing Japan to avoid a diversion of military power to the east.

A major source of strength for the Europe-first point of view developed in Army and Navy circles. In November of 1937 the Joint Army and Navy Board had begun work on a new Orange Plan for war with Japan to replace the obsolete plans which dated back to 1928. There was a strong reluctance to contemplate action in the western Pacific, the Philippines were generally recognized as indefensible, and the most effective weapon against Japan was considered by many to be a naval blockade. The outbreak of the war in Europe turned major attention to the Atlantic. The Army strongly opposed keeping the fleet at Hawaii, and in June, 1940, General George Marshall and Admiral Harold Stark secured President Roosevelt's agreement to transfer the main body of American naval power to the Atlantic if the French fleet passed to German control. By late 1940 General Marshall was writing: "A serious commitment in the Pacific is just what Germany would like to see us undertake." Admiral Stark was convinced that the soundest course of action was to remain on "a strict defensive" in the Pacific while preparing for land operations in Europe.

One of the strongest exponents of the Europe-first position in the Roosevelt cabinet was Secretary of the Treasury Henry Morgenthau. In the spring of 1941 Morgenthau's energetic assistant, Harry Dexter White, prepared a policy memorandum in which he attacked the problem of ambivalence and proposed a program to end the tension in the Pacific and to free American energies for the European conflict. White called for a two billion dollar credit to Japan, the abolition of the Japanese Exclusion Act, and tariff and trade concessions to Japan. In return the Japanese were to withdraw from China, keeping only enough troops in Manchuria to balance the Soviet forces on the border, and to make available to the United States for use in Europe three-fourths of Japan's current output of war matériel, to be paid for on a generous cost-plus-twenty-per-cent basis. Circulation of the White plan in government circles was delayed until November, 1941, when its reception demonstrated the strength of the Europe-first point of view. The chief of the Far Eastern Division, Maxwell Hamilton, with the concurrence of the senior members of his staff, concluded that this memorandum was "the most constructive one" he had seen. Admiral Stark considered it acceptable to the Navy with minor qualifications. General Lee Gerow, acting in General George Marshall's absence, said that the adoption of the White plan would attain "one of our present major objectives—the avoidance of war with Japan." Gerow had some qualifications, but he stressed that at least a *modus vivendi* should be reached with Japan.

In the cabinet, Secretary of War Stimson also gave some support to major emphasis on Europe. In May, 1941, he urged the President to issue an executive order which would bring the Pacific naval forces into the Atlantic. The President himself continued to speak of the Atlantic as having first priority. In a letter written on July 1, 1941, the President said: ". . . it is terribly important for the control of the Atlantic for us to help to keep the peace in the Pacific. I simply have not got enough Navy to go round—and every little episode in the Pacific means fewer ships in the Atlantic." In practice, however, the President soon took action which committed the United States to an Asia-first policy.

One of the strongest of the Asia-firsters was Stanley K. Hornbeck, Adviser on Political Relations. "Stanley regards Japan as the sun around which her satellites, Germany and Italy, were revolving," said a career American diplomat in October, 1940. Hornbeck's chief, Cordell Hull, seems also to have inclined to the same perspective on world affairs. After the fall of Austria in March, 1938, Secretary of Interior Ickes complained that Hull "seems to defer unduly to Hitler and Mussolini, while he all but rattles the saber when it comes to Japan." The President's adviser, Norman Davis, who sympathized with the Cliveden set's point of view on Germany, was another Asia-firster. An American diplomat, returning to Washington in the fall of 1940, found that of all the people with whom he talked Davis was "the one who would view a war with Japan with the greatest equanimity."

The thesis that aggression began and must be met first in Asia was disputed in the fall of 1941 by an eminent American scholar, A. Whitney Griswold. There were no longer any geographical or logical barriers between European and Asian wars, Griswold argued, but the time had come for "approaching the Far East via the front door of Europe, rather than, as in the old days, approaching Europe via the backdoor of the Far East." But the old method appealed for practical reasons to an increasingly belligerent member of the Roosevelt cabinet, Harold Ickes. The Secretary of Interior wrote in his diary in October, 1941:

For a long time I have believed that our best entrance into the war would be by way of Japan. . . . Japan has no friends in this country, but China has. And of course if we go to war against Japan, it will inevitably lead us into war against Germany.

Ickes was one of the strongest supporters of the President's executive order of July 26, 1941, freezing all Japanese assets in the United States and halting all trade. The Dutch and British joined in this order, which had the drastic effect of cutting off all Japan's oil and gasoline imports. The significance of this step in provoking Japan to take last-ditch countermeasures was grasped in military and naval circles. Ten days before the issuance of the order the War Plans Division had warned that an embargo on Japan would "possibly . . . involve the United States in early war in the Pacific." Both Admiral Stark and General Marshall opposed the Presidential order, but it was strongly advocated by Stanley Hornbeck, and inconsistently enough by Secretaries Morgenthau and Stimson.

Harold Ickes's conclusion that it would be easier for the United States to enter the European war via the Pacific seems to have been reached also by Winston Churchill. The British Prime Minister was clear about his own nation's priorities and placed resistance to Japan fourth; the defense of the homeland, the struggle in the Mediterranean and the Middle East, and aid to the Soviet Union all ranked higher in importance. But Churchill was frankly anxious to have the United States in the European conflict directly or via the Pacific: "If . . . Japanese aggression drew in America, I would be content to have it." The Prime Minister urged the President to join in an ultimatum to Japan against any southward moves.

Those members of the Roosevelt administration who continued to see Hitler as an enemy to be faced by a total concentration of American power made one more fight for their point of view. The White plan for a general settlement in the Pacific was finally watered down to a ten-point *modus vivendi* in which the *quid pro quo* was reduced to an offer to restore commercial relations with Japan and co-operation in helping Japan meet its economic needs in the East Indies. Even this mild effort to delay the breaking off of relations with Japan was rejected by the Asia-firsters.

Presidential adviser Lauchlin Currie maintained direct communication with Chiang Kai-shek's American adviser, Owen Lattimore, who in turn was able to present the Chinese position in the White House without going through the State Department. In mid-September, 1941, Lattimore had summarized the Chinese point of view for the President:

They want the war won first in Asia, leading after that to victory in Europe. . . . They also think that the East is the logical place to win the first stage of victory. . . in order to conserve their energy they want Japan defeated from the outside—by Britain, America, by Russia, by anybody.

When news of the proposed *modus vivendi* reached China in November, Lattimore informed the White House that he had never seen Chiang as "really agitated" as he was over this information. "Any *modus vivendi* now arrived at with Japan would be disastrous to Chinese belief in America," Lattimore advised. Churchill also threw his support in the move to scuttle this effort at a temporary settlement with Japan. "We certainly do not want an additional war," the British leader wired Washington, but "what about Chiang Kai-shek? Is he not having a very thin diet?"

The victory of the Asia-first line of thought on November 26 was described by Secretary Ickes in sympathetic terms: "The strong opposition of China and Britain caused the appeasers of the State Department to pause. They went to the White House and in the end the President refused to go through with the deal." Instead Japan received what Professor William Langer calls "the most uncompromising statement of American terms." Japan, as the President and his military chiefs agreed on November 25, could be expected to attack as early as November 30.

IV

Unity of objectives was not achieved in American foreign policy with Pearl Harbor; Germany's declaration of War on December 11, 1941, brought the United States into a two-front war where the desire for victory on both fronts produced new strains of ambivalence. The friends of China fought for major allocations of fighting power to the Pacific and for emphasis on direct aid to China itself. The influence of this point of view in Washington was noted by Winston Churchill, who, once the United States was in the European war, "found the extraordinary significance of China in American minds, even at the top, strangely out of proportion." The Prime Minister was offended to find that China was being accorded almost an equal fighting power with the British Empire. To General Wavell, Commander-in-Chief in India, Churchill wrote on January 23, 1942: "If I can epitomise in one word the lesson

I learned in the United States, it was 'China.' " Although Asia-firsters like Owen Lattimore continued to argue in 1943 that "the battlefield on which the Japanese are most vulnerable is the Chinese battlefield," the mainland of China never received high military priority. The precariousness of the supply lines, the difficulties of co-operation with Generalissimo Chiang, and commitment to the strategy of island-hopping prevented the war in the Pacific from being a China-first war. Chiang and his supporters had won a victory in November, 1941, but it was an empty triumph.

In the postwar world the battle of European and Asian interests took on new life within a changed framework. The rapid reconversion of the American image of Japan from enemy to ally, speeded by the success of Chinese communism, broke the traditional pattern of American thought about Asia. China, the keystone of American interest for a century or more, became a new nation. As diplomat John MacMurray predicted in 1935, the Chinese turned their backs upon the benevolent nation which destroyed the Japanese threat and looked to Moscow instead. What appeared to be abiding Chinese-American friendship was shattered, and the phrase "the Open Door in China" was erased from the vocabulary of American diplomacy. The United States experienced the most drastic diplomatic revolution of its history with domestic repercussions which produced almost endless political debates.

The failure of the American effort to preserve national interests in China involves forces beyond the scope of conventional political analysis. The blunders of individuals, the role of personal animosities and attachments, the ambiguities and ambivalences appear to be only surface phenomena produced by more profound irrationalities in American thought. The image of China has meant much more than the sum total of concrete national interests: investments, trade, missionary activities, and the like. China was in some respects a part of America's future, an element in a more sophisticated version of twentieth-century Manifest Destiny.

John Dewey in 1926 noted that "our concern with China is parental rather than economic." Dewey granted that even parental sentiments have economic elements, but denied that this was the essential element. Instead, America was a domineering but loving father, knowing what was best for the child and expecting lifelong gratitude in return. George Kennan touched on a similar irrational element in commenting on the tendency of Americans to "hazy and exalted dreams of intimacy with other peoples," particularly with peoples, like the Chinese, far from America geographically and culturally. Whatever the analogue which best describes this relationship, parental or conjugal, Americans assumed as a consequence their ability to exercise an effective guidance over the destinies of China's millions. "The key to the future of China," wrote a distinguished Far Eastern expert in 1940, "lies neither in Japan nor in Russia, nor even in China itself. It lies right here in America." When China turned to the Soviet Union for a political and economic pattern, a mood of bitterness touched many Americans. This deviation too must come of American doing, by blunder or treachery, and politicians set out to find the guilty individuals or individual.

Dreams of destiny dissolve slowly but surely. The same Far Eastern expert who in 1940 spoke so confidently about possessing the key to China's future was a wiser man in 1949. He expressed a more rational viewpoint when he interrupted a discussion in the State Department: "We have been talking about Asia, the American Problem. Since when and by whom was Asia given to America to solve its problems?" When and by whom Asia was given the United States is a pioneering area for exploration. Analysis of the psychological and sociological foundations of the concept of American destiny in the Far East may come closest to revealing the roots of failure for the American approach to Asia.

7. *Kenneth W. Thompson*

Isolationism and Collective Security:
The Uses and Limits of Two Theories of International Relations

The Citizens of the United States cherish sentiments the most friendly, in favor of the liberty and happiness of their fellowmen on that side of the Atlantic. In the wars of the European powers, in matters relating to themselves, we have never taken any part, nor does it comport with our policy, so to do. It is only when our rights are invaded, or seriously menaced, that we resent injuries, or make preparations for our defense.

JAMES MONROE, 1823

AMERICA's foreign relations are no exception to the cardinal rule that objective conditions largely shape and govern a nation's external relations. For approximately one hundred and thirty-four years, from the Treaty of Paris in 1783 until the First World War, the United States was relatively immune from the European struggle for power. This singular good fortune resulted from a convergence of at least three factors: America's geographical position and remoteness from Europe, the European balance of power, and the absence of strong and hostile neighbors. Even so, it must be noted that the United States fought two wars with its only powerful neighbor, Great Britain, and went to the brink with several others. Against our historic position, these misfortunes inspired the kind of caution reflected as late as June 2, 1937, by Secretary of State Cordell Hull, who told four members of the House of Representatives who visited him in connection with the application of the Neutrality Act to Germany and Italy: "This is not our war. We must be cautious. We must be quiet." His words suggest there is in each of us something of an isolationist.

What can we say about isolationism? Is it or has it ever been a carefully worked out philosophy or idea of international relations? Or is it primarily a national impulse reflecting the deeply felt but inchoate needs of the people? Or can we associate it with certain interest groups striving to assert and to rationalize their claims? Perhaps all three conditions are true but if we examine the roots of isolationism the emphasis will probably fall more on one than on the others.

One way of encompassing our problem and fencing it in may be by enumerating the elements of isolationism as they are writ large in recent American history. The first ingredient undoubtedly is the role of immigrant groups. They had shaken the dust of Europe from their feet and had crossed the Atlantic in the spirit of a "chosen people." They shared the intellectual and emotional tradition of men who have come out from a house of bondage into the "promised land." For them the dogma that they were not as other men was less an audacious paradox than an unquestioned truism. Their faith was reflected in a holy mission embodied in the century and a half of experience that served to confirm to a remarkable extent their underlying creed. This success was reinforced by the fact that sacred sentiments and hallowed traditions stand above and beyond discussion, self-criticism, and compromise. In this, we shall discover, isolationism and collective security have something basically in common.

The immigrant in American life becomes a particularly crucial factor if we accept the view that proclamations of isolationism increasingly were founded more upon an attitude and frame of mind than on any clear conception of America's international situation. Immigrants held to the common conviction that their new country was *alter orbis* and that it behooved them to demonstrate unquestioning fealty to their new sovereign. They were prone to accept the sometimes historically relevant description of Europe as a region of "ambition, rivalship, interest, humor, or caprice." Power politics was an invention of Western Europe which Europe's heirs on the shores of North America were expected to spurn.

A second factor which nurtured an isolationist outlook was the continuing appeal of an essentially libertarian and anti-militaristic conception of America's destiny. A succession of extremely able philosophers and writers found nonaggressive and abstentionist terms of reference to describe the nation's mission. Thus John C. Calhoun conceived that Americans would "do more to extend liberty by our example over this continent and the world generally, than would be done by a thousand victories." Protesting against the tendencies inherent in the Spanish-American War, William Graham Sumner wrote: "Expansion and imperialism are a grand onslaught on democracy ... [they] are at war with the best traditions, principles, and interests of the American people." Sumner saw European power politics as diametrically opposed to American ideals and heralded the Spanish-American War as the end of our cherished liberties. Indeed, the notion that isolation is the one means of preserving democracy runs like a red thread from the views of the founding Fathers to Senator Borah to Senator Robert A. Taft. It is clearly among the fundamentals of isolationist thought.

A corollary of this libertarian doctrine has been the emphasis on economics over politics. John Adams declared that he would lay down as a first principle of foreign policy that "we should calculate all our measures and foreign negotiations in such a manner, as to avoid too great dependence upon any power of Europe . . . that the business of America with Europe was commerce, not politics or war." The term "treaty" itself was used in an early period of American history less often as an indication of a political bond than in a *traité de commerce.* Franklin spoke of exchanging "commerce for friendship" and is reported to have offered the French agent in Philadelphia *"un commerce exclusif."* In the early days of the Revolution the colonies were dependent upon foreign aid and the greater part of their gunpowder came from across the seas. In March, 1776, Adams sketched out what he conceived as a proper form of alliance with France based upon the following formula: "1. No officers from her. 2. No military connection. Receive no troops from her. 3. Only a commercial connection; that is, make a treaty to receive her ships into our ports; let her engage to receive our ships into her ports; furnish us with arms, cannon, saltpetre, powder, duck and steel." The colonists in seeking to replace politics among nations with commerce between states were following eighteenth-century thought. They had learned from the *philosophes* the tradition which was to become one of the pillars on which isolationism was to rest—though one must hasten to add that this tradition equally supported at least one internationalist strain of thought. We must loook to this tradition, however, to understand the objects of government and of foreign policy at the founding of the Republic. They were purely and simply to protect the individual in the exercise of certain rights. The nation's soil must be safeguarded from military or political intrusion and citizens must be protected and assisted when their commercial, religious, or cultural activities spilled over national boundaries. These two functions—promoting national security and private American economic activities abroad—were all that flowed from the original objects of American society. This libertarian view was put forth in the 1920's again by men like Senators William Borah, Hiram Johnson, and George Norris. There were to be sure a limited group whose libertarianism took a different spirit of missionary zeal; they pursued as their goal the spread of "republicanism" as early as the Greek Rebellion in 1820-1830, and again in 1898. However, the main stream of libertarianism in the nineteenth and early twentieth centuries was pacifist and isolationist.

A third element, and perhaps the most basic, is the expansionist program which carried Americans westward across a vast continent that was virtually empty but enormously rich. From the French wars of the eighteenth century to the close of the nineteenth century, the American purpose was to open up a continental territory, to consolidate it within the Union, and to make it as invulnerable as possible against other powers. The struggle to secure a new continent officially ended only in

1890 with the close of the last of our thirty-seven wars with the Indians.

Ironically, the true believers in a policy of taming the continental domain are today called isolationists. Yet the memory of their struggles against foreign powers, the wilderness, and the Indians should make it plain that if they stood for anything it was not pacifism or withdrawal. The words of our early leaders—Washington, Adams, Monroe, and their successors—must be viewed in historical context. When Washington urged political separation from Europe, he was painfully aware that his new nation was surrounded by unfriendly foreign powers. It was to assure a free hand for expansion to the West that his successors frequently quoted the words of his Farewell Address: "The great rule of conduct for us in regard to foreign nations is in extending our commercial relations to have with them as little political connection as possible." Moreover, it was to bring about the evacuation of the last frontier post held by British soldiers on American soil and to assure the opening for settlement of the Ohio Valley that Washington defended the unpopular Jay Treaty. Expansionists in eighteenth- and nineteenth-century America wished to isolate the continental domain and the Western Hemisphere, to conquer it not as an empire but as "a new domicile of freedom,'" and to accomplish their ends not in response to domination by others but with freedom of action. The expansionist impulse carried Americans westward to the Pacific, where at the mid-nineteenth century they paused at the "water's edge."

It is curious how the expansionist urge has characterized both political parties in the United States. Even present-day Republicans, who until recently clung to isolationism, have been imperialists and interventionists in Asia. Their political predecessors—having presided over the setttlement and development of the West, consolidated the Union under Lincoln, and seen the frontiers disappear—were responsible in 1867 for the purchase of Alaska. They annexed Hawaii. They conquered the Philippines. They have provided their share of demagogues who exploited the aspirations of those looking westward to the promised land. The fervor of this expansionist program reduced the energy which could be directed to participation in European affairs.

Alongside the expansionist tradition there is also an anti-expansionist view. It reflects itself in the "little United States" line of thought deriving from Hamilton in the arguments, albeit constitutional, against the Louisiana Purchase, and in certain Whig attitudes about the Mexican War and against expansion in 1812. It may give us a clue to another, and partly contradictory, source of isolationism.

By referring to these three elements of isolationism—the role of immigrant or ethnic groups, the libertarian tradition, and westward expansion—we have of course hardly made contact with the central problem of the existence of a theory of isolationism. Indeed in one sense it is futile to talk of a theory of isolationism, for the term is charged with emotion and has increasingly acquired pejorative connotations. Isolationism and the mythology surrounding it suggest inaction, passivity, lethargy, and withdrawal. Is it any wonder that those who espouse isolationism prefer to be called nationalists, continentalists, or even "America Firsters"? If isolationism is seldom if ever professed, but rather ascribed or imputed to objects of attack, a coherent, self-conscious and self-critical theory seems almost by definition beyond reach. Isolationism is not a theory but a predicament, we are told. Or it is useful "only insofar as it indicates the misunderstanding of an ideology, serves as a point of departure for investigation, and contains in its connotations certain suggestive half-truths."

These criticisms and impressions suggest that, whereas isolationism may be either an impulse or the reflection of interests or interest groups, it is surely not a theory. Before we accept this judgment, however, we should perhaps look a little further. It may be that we shall find a deposit of ideas, beliefs, and values that can be analyzed and assessed.

The historian of isolation, Alfred Weinberg, has written: "In all seriousness, isolation is not a theory of American foreign policy. Isolation is a theory about a theory of American foreign policy." Who coined the word? If we view isolation in strictest terms, Washington can hardly be called its father. He warned against too much *political* connection, but this scarcely inhibited him from agreements respecting commerce and trade nor did it stand in the way of completing an alliance with France. Following Washington, few of his successors harked back to an avowedly isolationist course, although Seward spoke of the first President's counsel as one of isolation if "superficially viewed." For the most part, not the advocates of a policy of self-limitations but their opponents, seeking to discredit them, made a doctrine out of isolationism—criticizing, for example, those who opposed crusades like mid-nineteenth-century support of the revolutionary liberalism of Europe. The reserve of the isolationists was exaggerated and made into a weapon of political warfare.

Perhaps the core idea of isolationism is what has been called "national reserve," or "a deliberate and more or less regular abstention from certain political relationships." Plainly such a concept is not an American invention. It has many parallels, among them the "Little England" movement in the nineteenth century. It has roots in the universal human desire to think first about things nearest home. It amounts to the nonjuridical side of sovereignty. It finds expression wherever sovereign states seek maximum self-determination or freedom of action. Its American version, however, has accented aspects that are not everywhere stressed. Take for example nonentanglement. Self-determination ideally, in a world devoid of conflicts, might entitle a state to freedom from all alien interference. In the real world, it oftentimes requires treaties of mutual aid or alliances designed to safeguard independence itself. Because of America's geographical detachment, the place of alliances seemed distant and remote. Gradually this antipathy and suspicion of treaties spilled over into resistance to every source of entanglement, including policies designed to promote commerce which might be expected to lead to political contacts or to parallel but independent foreign policies of two or more states. Nonentanglement was possible for a country in the Western Hemisphere, but, with rare exceptions, for nation-states squeezed together in the heart of Europe it would have destroyed independence and with it all "freedom of action." What would have happened, for example, to the states making up a coalition against Napoleon if they had maintained that sovereignty involved freedom from all entangling alliances? Certain basic assumptions underlying America's approach to foreign policy, such as confidence in our self-sufficiency, a belief in the divergence of our interests from those of others, and a sense of moral and political superiority, gave an unique flavor to American isolationism. There was a residual deposit of ideas, about which we shall have more to say later, which formed the theoretical basis of our isolationism. But instead of bringing these concepts to the surface, giving them their due, and adapting them to changing circumstances, both friends and foes of isolation saw fit to erect such temporary expedients or instruments of isolationism as "nonentanglement" into ends or absolutes in themselves.

There are other examples of ideas and policies that may have served the basic idea of reserve and freedom of action but are scarcely equivalent. Nonintervention became such a doctrine for some American makers of policy who defined it *in extremis* to mean any trespass upon the external or internal sovereignty of others not warranted by a life-or-death-defense of our most vital interests. Underlying this was a fear of counterintervention and obsession with the perils of being caught up in the swift currents of international life. International law and its rules respecting intervention figured less prominently.

The problem of a theory of isolationism is therefore fraught with difficulties and pathos. There is a central idea that supports all the partial insights we have mentioned. It is in effect the concept Washington enunciated when he spoke about retaining "command of our fortunes." Its servants are policies of "reserve." Yet in American foreign relations this idea has expressed itself in a variety of creeds and dogmas which include "noninterference and nonparticipation in European

politics," "avoidance of joint action," "insulation against entanglement," and the other principles cited above. Moreover,
these limited concepts were sanctified and encrusted with
tradition until they were no longer conceived as "counsels of
prudence." They hardened into iron rules for conduct. The
manifold ingredients making up isolationism prevented the isolationist from looking for consistency and opposed the crystal-
lizing of a perceptive thory. It made isolationism a "happy
hunting ground" for politicians and invited fierce and impas-
sioned debate instead of reasoned analysis. Writing of the
so-called theory, one scholar has noted: "Because this interpretation is a poor theory, misrepresentative even if taken only
semi-literally, it has placed the discussion of American foreign policy on a bad predicament of obfuscation, not without
its influence upon national decisions."

In consequence we are likely to find the mainsprings of
isolationism in the play of national impulse and of interest and
ethnic groups. This is a theme that runs through Professor
DeConde's chapter and is one which in its myriad complexity
deserves the careful analysis and attention he gives to it. Our
purpose here is merely to suggest that as a theory isolationism
was deficient not because it lacked certain residual truths but
as a result of the way in which these truths were restricted and
exploited in political practice. As a result anti-European and
more particularly anti-English sentiment—most notably expressed by the Irish, the Germans, and the Swedes—was more
important than any rational set of isolationist ideals. It has been
well said: "Isolationism as a whole was not a constant force
nor a stable doctrine with a unique ideology. It fluctuated in
response to given situations and reflected ideas and attitudes of
differing groups which espoused it." One might add that these
ideas tended to calcify, making difficult the rapid shifts and
adjustments of policies that were required.

There was a final weakness preventing the emergence of
a rational theory of isolationism which would do justice equally
to the uniformities, ambiguities, and complexities of international life. This weakness may be illustrated by a reference

to the late Senator Robert A. Taft. If any isolationist or neo-
isolationist might have been expected to leave an enduring
legacy of isolationist theory, it would be a man of Taft's in-
telligence and integrity. Yet one looks in vain for consistency
and coherence in the foreign policies he embraced. Prior to
the Second World War, he held to a policy of neutrality,
maintaining that we had nothing to fear from Germany or from
the deterioration of the European situation. He predicted
that the outcome of a war in Europe would have no bearing on
American security; we could easily defend ourselves. Yet
the logic of his position was undermined by his support for
substantial and ever-increasing defense costs and was eventually
destroyed by his championing of aid to Britain. (He insisted
he had favored a loan to Britain, Canada, and Greece amount-
ing to two billion dollars before lend-lease "was ever introduced
or invented.") This in spite of repeated denials that American
security was bound up in any way with that of England. The
touchstone of Taft's foreign policy before the Second World
War was his fond hope that the United States be left alone.

Beginning in 1944, Taft became one of the most enthusiastic
supporters of a new international organization. Moreover,
he demanded that a "United Nations" be capable of solving
disputes by judicial process. At the same time he favored the
veto and challenged any diminution of sovereignty. If in
this unhappy state of affairs disputes proved not to be susceptible
of judicial solution, he preferred that we isolate ourselves
from them. He appeared to assume that the cause of justice
would be strengthened more by our doing nothing than by
our doing the best we could in an unsatisfactory situation. These
internal conflicts and inconsistencies reached a climax as Taft
became the leader of the opposition. During Truman's administrations he was endlessly critical but rarely constructive. He
was against the size of defense spending, whether eleven or
forty billion dollars were involved. He opposed increase of
European defense forces on grounds that the Soviet Union
might be provoked, but favored a more decisive Far Eastern
military campaign on grounds that there could be "no possible

threat" to Russia "from anything we may do in China." John P. Armstrong sums up his excellent study of Taft by noting: "His [Taft's] ideas fit no recognizable pattern; there is neither a consistent body of ideas bearing directly on the problem of foreign policy nor a progression from one position to another."

Yet if Taft's ideas on foreign policy were inconsistent, "what he had to say about the domestic consequences of foreign policy had a coherence, a consistency, and almost a rigidity." Whereas for many of our historic Western writers and statesmen the primacy of foreign policy over domestic policies and consequences was widely accepted, for Senator Taft the direct opposite was true. He took his stand for a strong legislature and a maximum of personal and economic freedom. He directed his wrath against big government, a strong executive, and high taxes. When he questioned lend-lease it was mainly in terms of the power it assigned the President. He opposed compulsory military service not because world political conditions made it unnecessary but out of concern that it might destroy democratic government. He came to attack President Truman's decision in Korea not because he questioned the soundness of such a policy but because in his mind it represented a usurpation of executive power.

If this can be said of a political leader with the extraordinary intellectual endowments of Senator Taft, it must be obvious that the theoretical foundations of isolationism are impoverished indeed. In a word, the problem of isolationism has been that, lacking roots in an enduring theory, it has taken root in *ad hoc* strategies and policies cast in the form of principles such as nonintervention and nonentanglement. Like plants artificially preserved long after they have withered and died, these policies as time has gone on have been confused with the theory in itself and come to claim the homage, devotion, and loyalty that broader precepts should command. The deposit of political truths that surrounded isolationism in an era when it formed a viable foreign policy was in consequence obscured and concealed from those who rushed in to supply a new theory. Perhaps partly because of the excesses and rigidities of isolationists, the proponents of collective security lost sight of the changeless truths underlying this ancient creed and in so doing perpetrated a new philosophy rooted less in impulse than theory—but a theory distorted, exaggerated, and ultimately enfeebled by its own excessive rationalism and utopianism. When we have held this new theory up to the mirror of reality, we shall in conclusion return to the lessons of isolationism seen in relation to those of collective security.

I

From one standpoint it is a truism to say that collective security is something new under the sun. In past eras, and especially in the eighteenth and nineteenth centuries, war was conceived of as a duel in which contestants should be isolated and restrained by the rest of international society. When nations engaged in armed conflict, their neighbors sought to localize the struggle and alleviate its poisonous effects. However short-sighted their actions in not meeting the conflict directly and turning back aggression at its source, the nations pursuing these policies were sometimes sucessful for varying periods of time in preserving islands of peace in a warring world.

On August 8, 1932, however, Secretary of State Henry L. Stimson proclaimed that the modern state system was entering a new era in which warring powers were no longer entitled to the same equally impartial and neutral treatment by the rest of society. He announced to the New York Council of Foreign Relations that in future conflicts one or more of the combatants must be designated as wrongdoer and added: "We no longer draw a circle about them and treat them with punctilios of the duelist's code. Instead we denounce them as lawbreakers."

This is the cornerstone of the almost universally recognized theory of collective security to which most Western statesmen profess loyalty today. It is said that Stimson's memoirs, *On Active Service*, have become the "bible" of the Department of State, and in Britain we have the word of the *Times* (London) in a recent editorial that collective security "indeed, is the view to which this country, like most others, is committed by its membership in the United Nations."

It is important that we ask at the outset, then: What is collective security in theory? What are its precepts and main tenets? What, in simplest terms, is the philosophy of collective security? The rock-bottom principle upon which collective security is founded provides that an attack on any one state will be regarded as an attack on all states. It finds its measure in the apparently simple doctrine of one for all and all for one. War anywhere, in the context of Article 11 of the League of Nations, is the concern of every state.

Self-help and neutrality, it should be obvious, are the exact antithesis of such a theory. States under an order of neutrality are impartial when conflict breaks out, give their blessing to combatants to fight it out, and defer judgment regarding the justice or injustice of the cause involved. Self-help in the past was often "help yourself" so far as the great powers were concerned; they enforced their own rights and more besides. In the eighteenth and nineteenth centuries this system was fashionable; and wars, although not eliminated, were localized whenever possible. In a more integrated world, a conflict anywhere has some effect on conditions of peace everywhere. Disturbance at one point upsets equilibrium at other points, and the adjustment of a single conflict restores the foundations of harmony throughout the world.

This idea of collective security is simple, challenging, and seemingly novel. It would do for the international society what police action does for the domestic community. If the individual is threatened or endangered in municipal society, he turns to the legitimate agents of law enforcement, the police. The comparatively successful operation of this system has meant relative peace and tolerable harmony for most local communities. Through the action of police or "fire brigades" on a world scale, collective security has as its goal two comparable objectives. It would prevent war by providing a deterrent to "aggression." It would defend the interest of "peace-loving" states in war if it came, by concentrating preponderance of power against the "aggressor."

This ideal of collective security nowhere has been taken more seriously than among responsible leaders in the United States. More than the other political leaders accountable for the conduct of national policies during and following the First World War, Woodrow Wilson assumed that national interests were rapidly being supplanted by the common enlightened purposes of mankind everywhere and, particularly at the outset of the peace talks, sought to act upon his convictions. But the moral and political foundations required for collective action vanished with cessation of hostilities and Wilson himself was forced to turn from his principles. He was driven to accept postwar territorial settlements in the Balkans that were at best half-hearted compromises with the crusade he had led. The tragic march of events of the Twenty Years' Crisis following 1919 revived the flame of belief in the hearts of other American political leaders that better forms for the conduct of international relations must be discovered and instituted. An uneasy conscience over America's departure from collective security after the First World War—when the Senate defeated the Covenant of the League of Nations—coupled with a more skilful marshaling of opinion in support of the United Nations, inspired internationalist and isolationist senators to support the same principle after the Second World War. In his first speech to the Senate, Harry S. Truman of Missouri declared: "The breaking of the peace anywhere is the concern of peace-loving nations everywhere." Following the San Francisco Conference, Senator Arthur H. Vandenberg announced in a dramatic speech to the Senate that he would support the ratification of the Charter with all the resources at his command. For, he explained, "peace must not be cheated of its collective chance. . . . We must have collective security to stop the next war, if possible, before it starts; and we must have collective action to crush it swiftly if it starts in spite of our organized precautions."

Indeed, American support for the new method of preserving international peace and order has gone considerably beyond the ritualism of pious affirmation of an inspiring ideal. Approval for the principles of collective security at the time of the Second World War was asserted even more eloquently in the actions and policies of its leaders. As a young man, Franklin D. Roosevelt had argued against the annexation of Hawaii. For, he maintained, "before we bother about foreign coaling-stations and fortifications we should look to the defense of our own coasts." New York, Boston, and San Francisco seemed still at the mercy of an enemy, and rather than prepare far-reaching security plans, the United States, he believed, ought to concentrate on its own national defenses. In his concrete policies, however, President Roosevelt rejected this youthful counsel. In the late 1930's, it became obvious to many informed leaders that American interests could be protected only if other nations were secure, and the Roosevelt foreign policy gradually became one of collective self-help. "Suppose my neighbor's home catches fire, and I have a length of garden hose," he remarked, in justifying Lend-Lease legislation to the Senate and the American people. This neighborly analogy was a practical way of convincing the people that their security was intimately bound up with Britain's struggle for survival.

This simple picture of the idea of collective security hardly furnishes a useful and realistic perspective on the way such a system operates in practice today. Nor are we helped by comparing the structure of the two historic experiments in collective security. The formal agencies for collective security after the First World War were in several important respects unimpressive. Article 16 of the Covenant provided that any member resorting to war contrary to the Covenant had committed *ipso facto* an act of aggression against all other members. It was intended that first economic measures and then overt force be applied against any offender. But although the international obligations of members were less ambiguous than in the Charter, there was no clear provision for their enforcement by a central agency. Each nation had full freedom to provide what troops it saw fit. The Council could then advise on additional measures. In contrast, Article 39 of the Charter of the United Nations commissions the Security Council to determine the existence of a threat to the peace or act of aggression and Articles 43-47 obligate the members, upon the completion of agreements, to supply troops to the Military Staff Committee. The agencies for partial collective security, as found in the constitutional provisions of the North Atlantic Pact and the practical steps undertaken under NATO are even more impressive.

From the beginning, however, the real issue concerning collective security has had little to do with charters or compacts. The real issue has been the question of why a system which to its supporters appeared logically so flawless, enjoying such impressive official devotion and popular support, should have been accompanied by a period of virtually unprecedented collective insecurity. It is a sobering fact that the nineteenth century was perhaps the most peaceful of modern centuries; the twentieth, by contrast, has been an epoch of unparalleled bloodshed. From 1815 to 1914 a system of old-fashioned balance of power contributed to the achievement of nearly a full century of uninterrupted peace. The past forty years have witnessed in rapid succession two great wars which the historian Arnold J. Toynbee compares to the double wars of the Romans and the Carthaginians and the two struggles of the Peloponnesian War which wrecked Hellenic civilization. He has observed that quite possibly we have dealt ourselves the same "knock-out blows" that these wars represented for the older civilizations. There were only eighteen months in this period from 1815 in the nineteenth century when France, Russia, Austria, Prussia, England, and Spain found themselves at war with one another (excluding the Crimean War as a colonial struggle). By contrast, our experience thus far with the novel machinery of collective security has hardly warranted the unqualified postwar optimism of men like Cordell Hull who believed that with the new international organizations, power politics and war were being left far behind in our progress toward utopia.

The recent decades have been years of unceasing war or threats of war. What are the causes of this state of affairs? What are the reasons for the enormous gap between theory and practice, promise and performance of collective security? The most popular and reassuring answer has been that the radical doctrines of National Socialism and Communism have undermined the ideal system, and that modern technology has shattered the earlier limitations on conflict. Yet an equally moving and dynamic creed—nationalism and the revolutionary tradition—challenged peace and order in the nineteenth century and provided a fighting faith for imperialist France. The serious observer must look to the basic requirements on which the new system has ostensibly been founded.

First, collective enforcement assumes a *status quo*, or situation of peace, on which the nations with predominant strength agree. In practical terms, the peace which a collective system must defend is the territorial *status quo* existing at the time the system is brought into being. Yet there is nothing in past experience to indicate that all nations, or even a combination sufficiently powerful to defy the rest, will agree on the meaning of a particular *status quo*. Following every war, the defeated powers who feel they have suffered most by the terms of peace come to oppose the established *status quo*. In the aftermath of the Second World War, however, the question of satisfaction or dissatisfaction with the *status quo* has largely been superseded by an earlier and prior question. Up to the present time, no practical arrangement has been worked out acceptable to the major powers, who in this case are primarily the Soviet Union and the United States, on which the postwar *status quo* could be founded. The unresolved conflict between East and West has prevented the establishment of peace. Consequently, the latest experiment in collective security presents us with the anomalous picture of a system created to defend a *status quo* which has not yet been brought into being.

Second, collective security demands that nations subscribing to the *status quo* be willing and able at all times to muster overwhelming strength for collective defense at successive points of conflict. In theory, the supporters of the *status quo* might be capable in particular emergencies of mobilizing effective and decisive power against the single aggressor who sought to defy them. Or by pooling the resources of all the nations in a permanently organized international force, collective enforcement could be made automatic, instantaneous, and preponderant. The former condition is practically impossible of fulfilment, inasmuch as the threat to the *status quo* comes historically from more than one dissatisfied power or aggressor. The second condition would call for the unprecedented practice of international contingents operating under an international agency empowered to decide when and how they should be used.

The United Nations Charter seemingly moves a long step toward this objective by providing that all members are "to make available to the Security Council, on its call and in accordance with a special agreement or agreements, armed forces, assistance and facilities" (Article 43, Paragraph 1). Through this provision, the incurable weakness of decentralized enforcement by which past international systems have been rendered impotent is ostensibly rectified. For the Achilles' heel of the earlier experiments was the decentralized character of the enforcement process: separate nations retained the right to determine whether or not military forces would be made available to meet particular crises. Cordell Hull in 1942 had urged that "some international agency must be created which can— by force, if necessary—keep the peace." Yet Hull's proposition and Articles 43 ff. of the Charter, by which this historic difficulty apparently had been surmounted, in practice have until recently remained dead letters. The Soviet Union has opposed proportionate contributions to an international air and naval force, which would leave it particularly vulnerable to forces overwhelmingly more powerful than its own. The United States has been concerned to make the United Nations armed forces as strong as possible against the preponderance of the Soviet Army in Europe and Asia, while the Russians have sought to keep them as weak as possible. Even recent developments in Egypt leave the future of an international police force to be used against major as well as second-rate powers quite unclear. In practice, realization of the second condition of overwhelming strength for collective enforcement has constantly run afoul of special national demands for military security and supremacy.

There is a third and final prerequisite. It is essential to collective security in a world of unequal powers that at least the major powers enjoy a minimum of political solidarity and moral community. On October 13, 1944, Premier Stalin asked himself, in an article appearing in the Soviet *Information Bulletin*, if the world organization could be effective. He predicted that it would "be effective if the Great Powers, which have borne the brunt of the war against Hitler-Germany, continue to act in a spirit of unanimity and accord."

The effectiveness of the United Nations and of the Security Council in particular was predicated upon the unanimity of the five great powers. It was an article of political faith in the Roosevelt Administration that trustworthiness and good will on the part of Americans would inspire the same qualities among the Russians. In a particularly revealing memorandum for President Harry S. Truman dated September 11, 1945, Stimson explained: "The chief lesson I have learned in a long life is that the only way you can make a man trustworthy is to trust him; and the surest way to make him untrustworthy is to distrust him and show your distrust." Unanimity among the great powers, which alien ideologies and conflicting interests might otherwise undermine, would be secured through the application of a code of social ethics that had been effective within the United States.

By October, 1947, Stimson, writing in *Foreign Affairs*, had cause to reformulate his proposition. "I have often said that the surest way to make a man trustworthy is to trust him. But I must add that this does not always apply to a man who is determined to make you his dupe. Before we can make friends with the Russians, their leaders will have to be convinced that they have nothing to gain, and everything to lose, by acting on the assumption that our society is dying and that our principles are outworn." Thus the conditions of collective security under the United Nations have either been wanting from the beginning, or have been corroded and destroyed by the all-consuming forces of the "cold war." Yet the chief practical obstacle to collective security is the political problem deriving from the conflict of independent foreign policies. The loyalties and interests of nations participating in international organizations and systems of collective security are of a different order from those of individuals taking part in the more intimate communities of the family and nation. Some years ago Paul Henri Spaak in an address before the Foreign Press Union declared:

There must me a hierarchy in international obligations. The nations of the continent cannot be asked to consider with the same realism and sincerity of judgment affairs which directly concern them and events which are taking place thousands of kilometres away in regions where they have neither interests nor influence. Indivisible peace, mutual assistance, and even collective security are general ideas whose practical effect must be clearly explained and clearly limited.

Both individuals and nations pursue their own interests, but in some areas and on certain occasions the individual may forsake his egotistic motives for loyalty to some higher institution or nobler cause. There are institutions in integrated societies which provide common standards under which the individual can realize his aspirations. There need be no inherent conflict between an individual's private interest and his national loyalties, for the latter can often promote the realization of the former. On the other hand, conflicts are often inevitable between national and supranational loyalties, and when the projected policy of an international organization conflicts with that of a particular nation, the national interest prevails.

In the debate between the so-called realists and idealists, the latter have often assumed that the conflict between national and supranational policies and purposes need not take

the form the realists give it.   Idealists have maintained that
if two sets of objectives should be in conflict, the clash could
always be resolved by taking "the long view."   It should not
be surprising that statesmen have been disposed to approach
the foreign policies of nations other than their own with this
as their "rule of thumb."   For example, on January 10, 1945,
in a speech before the Senate, Arthur H. Vandenberg assessed the objectives of the Soviet Union.   He announced that
the Soviet leaders appeared to contemplate the engulfment,
directly or indirectly, of a surrounding circle of states on the
Russian borders.   Their defense of this sphere-of-influence
policy was on grounds of security against German aggression.
While finding this a perfectly understandable claim, Senator
Vandenberg observed:

The alternative is collective security. . . . Which is better in the long
view, from a purely selfish Russian standpoint: To forcefully surround
herself with a cordon of unwillingly controlled or partitioned states, thus
affronting the opinion of mankind . . . or to win the priceless asset of
world-confidence in her by embracing the alternative, namely, full and
whole hearted cooperation with and reliance upon a vital international
organization.

Yet Senator Vandenberg and other American statesmen,
while raising this standard for others, have by their actions
and, not infrequently, by their words appealed to another less
lofty, if more attainable, goal.   Not all of our leaders have
been as transparently candid as Senator Vandenberg in expressing the hope that "American spokesmanship at the peace table
is at least as loyal to America's own primary interests as Mr.
Stalin is certain to be in respect to Russia and Mr. Churchill
. . . to the British Empire."   Still in his warning the Senator
appeared to employ a second "rule of thumb" based on the
precept "that no one is going to look out for us . . . unless we
look out for ourselves."

III

Looking back over the past forty years we can say that isolationism and collective security as major trends in America's

foreign relations have shared certain qualities in common. Neither had any absolute value; each influenced the other in American practice. One or both appear to have suffered from a high rate of obsolescence. Each was founded on partly dubious assumptions. For example, collective security implies that relations with a possible aggressor state are such that there can be no doubt as to right or wrong. It assumes that the members of security agencies are not associated with the possible aggressor (cf. France and Italy at the time of Ethiopia) in any of those complicated relations out of which can grow conflicting views on the threat to vital interests. Isolationism in turn has its peculiar perils. Its apparent stress on the primacy of the national interest and the right of a state in this troubled world to retain control over its own destiny is for the foreseeable future a valid and neglected truth. Yet the national interest for isolationists is identified traditionally with the emotions and impulses now of particular ethnic groups and again of chosen economic or intellectual elites within the nation. Seldom has the isolationist proceeded from an objective appraisal of our vital interests, distribution of power in the world, and the resulting threat to American security. This may be true again today in the interservice dispute involving Admiral Arthur W. Radford and his colleagues. Someone responsible for foreign policy, looking dispassionately at the continuation of conflict in the world, might conclude that wars in some form are inevitable. He might decide, however, that an exception could be atomic or hydrogen conflicts. Preparing in part for the worst through some emphasis on new weapons, he might at the same time insist that conventional military forces should be kept in a state of readiness to meet limited conflicts. In truth, both prudence and recent history in Korea and Indo-China lend support to this approach. We may ask then whether the type of mentality which insists that American military preparations should be designed exclusively for the absolute struggle is not in a sense a latter-day version of isolationism. Is the one-shot approach to global conflict a case of having everything rather than nothing to do with the world and having done with it as quickly as possible? Can we define neo-isolationism as isolationism turned inside out? Is it a matter of isolating the making of decisions in foreign policy from the endless pressures and contacts of other sovereign states, rather than insulating the Western Hemisphere as in the past? Is it having everything rather than nothing to do with the world—but on one's own terms?

In the final analysis, perhaps isolationism and collective security threaten to mislead us because of their dismissal of politics with its uncertainties, its limited actions, and its tactics of advance and retreat. The one boasts a heritage, kept alive by the passion of ethnic minorities striving valiantly to prove their Americanism, which identifies politics, compromise and adjustment in diplomacy, and alliances with the decadence and corruption of Europe. Despite the rich intellectual resources devoted to its defense, isolationism has failed to supply a lasting and viable theory of international relations. It has sacrificed its command of certain residual truths by clinging to the form rather than the substance of freedom of action. For command of one's fortunes, in a nation as in a family, can never be absolute. It requires a recognition of certain mutualities of interests without sacrificing what is essential. Isolation gives us no theory of international politics because in fact it has been indifferent to international politics with its uncertain terrain, its dilemmas and tragic compromises, its ambiguities, half-truths, and shades of gray, and its inevitable stress on abhorrent terms like power and national interest.

But for different reasons collective security has failed us, has left us with problems it could never solve, and has preserved and increased the gap already existing between theory and practice. It has approached foreign policy dogmatically and legalistically rather than pragmatically. While isolation provides no theory, collective security gives us a philosophy so abstract and idealized as to provide little guidance in practice. To make collective security effective even in the most modest way, the policy-maker in any instance would have to ask a series of questions: Is overt military aggression the main thing to be feared? Are the methods prescribed to counter it ones likely to be disruptive to the power of resistance to other forms of aggression? Is it possible to define acts of aggression in a manner agreed to by all the members of the coalition? Is the *status quo* to be preserved by collective security capable of and worth preserving, or is it likely to come apart at the seams despite all efforts?

When such questions are answered in each emerging case, the value of collective security can be gauged. Clearly the moral is that collective security as a means of achieving world peace is no more an absolute than arbitration or disarmament or the outlawry of war. Its positive value may sometimes be very great, but this will depend on a whole series of specific variables which cannot be brought under the control of any fixed theoretical concept. It is unhappily the case that however persistently men may seek for some blanket code of procedural rules, compliance with a code would automatically do away with such realities as the immense variety of the human family, the inescapable conflicts of its members as they seek influence and power, and the fact that human behavior is only partially calculable by man himself, by reason of the fact that he lacks both the means and the moral courage fully to understand himself.

If collective security is insufficient as a theory of international relations, it may nonetheless have its place if applied judiciously and with immense reserve and self-restraint. It can be a means of organizing and making legitimate the network of mutual interests of a "free-world" coalition, especially if the task of preserving the tenuous ties among them is taken seriously. This calls for the best arts of statecraft and diplomacy, arts which antedate collective security by centuries. I have suggested in another connection that

Perhaps the supreme paradox of American foreign policy today is the necessity placed upon us to seize and employ the essentially utopian instruments of collective security in a brutally realistic power struggle. Its agencies furnish a political framework through which the broad coalition of the free world can be strengthened and a more stable equilibrium of world power be restored.   Britain and France and the free powers of Asia are more likely to play their part and contribute to the restoration of a balance of power in Asia if we assure them support through mutual guarantees and create confidence by discussion in the halls and anterooms of the United Nations.

Three years later I would add only that for every concrete policy the value of the consolidation of the "free world" must be measured coolly and dispassionately against the effects on our ties with the neutral and uncommitted nations.   In certain cases they may yearn more for economic aid or political recognition than mutual guarantees.   Thus an empirical and pragmatic approach, as against a legalistic and punitive view of collective security, finds uses more modest and limited than the ardent advocates assume.   It is but one variable among many.   It aims at the institutionalizing of force but perhaps must settle for the facilitating of a more stable balance of power.   Today's realities are such that it should be played in a minor key as against economic growth, peaceful change, and the harmonizing of differences.   Tomorrow's facts could call for new estimates and insights.   Until then perhaps we should safeguard and preserve the recurring truths we find at the heart of isolationism and collective security, however inadequate, until we have a more inclusive and recognized body of theory for American foreign policy.

Bibliographical Notes

While these essays rely on a wide variety of scattered sources, primary and secondary, they are essentially introductions to their subjects and make no pretense at being comprehensive. The references cited bear most directly on the subjects of the essays and are usually representative of a larger literature. Most of the sources cited contain further bibliographical references.

Chapter 1

ON TWENTIETH-CENTURY ISOLATIONISM

There is no general study of twentieth-century isolationism, particularly of its ideas, but for the general background of nineteenth-century isolation there are three fundamental studies. The latest is Albert K. Weinberg, "The Historical Meaning of the American Doctrine of Isolation," *American Political Science Review*, XXXIV (April, 1940), 539-547. J. Fred Rippy wrote two monographs, *America and the Strife of Europe* (Chicago, 1938) and, with Angie Debo, "The Historical Background of the American Policy of Isolation," *Smith College Studies in History*, IX, Nos. 3 and 4 (Northampton, Mass., April and July, 1924). William L. Langer in "Diplomatic Isolation," *Encyclopaedia of the Social Sciences*, VIII, 352-355 has placed isolation in a world-wide diplomatic context. Thomas A. Bailey in *The Man in the Street* (New York, 1948) has several chapters on the "roots" and "fruits" of isolationism and Thomas I. Cook and Malcolm Moos in *Power through Purpose: The Realism of Idealism as a Basis for Foreign Policy* (Baltimore, 1954) analyze isolationism in broad general terms and equate isolation with "insulationism."

A book which covers isolationism in a large setting is Foster Rhea Dulles, *America's Rise to World Power: 1898-1954* (New York, 1955), and another which deals with isolationism and ideas is Robert

E. Osgood, *Ideals and Self-Interest in America's Foreign Relations* (Chicago, 1953). Useful also is Selig Adler, "Isolationism since 1914," *The American Scholar*, XXI (Summer, 1952), 335-344. For the works of isolationists themselves several of the books of Charles A. Beard express the isolationist viewpoint; conveniently short and clear is his *A Foreign Policy for America* (New York, 1940). Another representative isolationist work is Arthur H. Vandenberg, *The Trail of a Tradition* (New York, 1926).

Among more special studies the following are rewarding. Samuel Lubell, in *The Future of American Politics* (New York, 1952) and *Revolt of the Moderates* (New York, 1956), offers a stimulating interpretation of ethnic and sectional isolationism, as does Ray Allen Billington in "Origins of Middle Western Isolationism," *Political Science Quarterly*, LX (March, 1945), 44-64; also Ralph H. Smuckler, "The Region of Isolationism," *American Political Science Review*, XLVII (June, 1953), 386-401. For a provocative study on sectional influence in foreign policy see Richard W. Leopold, "The Mississippi Valley and American Foreign Policy, 1890-1941: An Assessment and an Appeal," *Mississippi Valley Historical Review*, XXXVII (March, 1951), 625-642. For studies of the South in foreign policy there is Wayne S. Cole, "America First and the South, 1940-1941," *Journal of Southern History*, XXII (Feb., 1956), 36-47; Marian D. Irish, "Foreign Policy and the South," *Journal of Politics*, X (May, 1948), 306-326; and Virginius Dabney, "The South Looks Abroad," *Foreign Affairs*, XIX (Oct., 1940), 171-178.

For the reaction of selected intellectuals to isolationism, see William T. Hutchinson, "The American Historian in Wartime," *Mississippi Valley Historical Review*, XXIX (Sept., 1949), 163-186. Eric Goldman in *Rendezvous with Destiny: A History of Modern American Reform* (New York, 1952) analyzes liberal isolationism. For isolationism prior to the Second World War, Walter Johnson's *The Battle against Isolation* (Chicago, 1944) should be read together with Wayne S. Cole's *America First: The Battle against Intervention, 1940-1941* (Madison, 1953). Harry Elmer Barnes, ed., in *Perpetual War for Perpetual Peace* (Caldwell, Idaho, 1953), has brought together the views of prominent revisionists of the Second World War.

Henry A. Wallace's *Toward World Peace* (New York, 1948) and Robert A. Taft's *A Foreign Policy for Americans* (New York, 1951) are unique sources for the isolationism of the 1940's and 1950's. For the same period see also Adlai E. Stevenson, "The Challenge of a New Isolationism," *New York Times Magazine* (Nov. 6, 1949), p. 9; Arthur M. Schlesinger, Jr., "The New Isolationism," *Atlantic Monthly*, CLXXXIX (May, 1952), 34-38; and especially Norman A. Graebner's *The New Isolationism: A Study in Politics and Foreign Policy Since 1950* (New York, 1956).

Chapter 2

THE UNITED STATES AND "COLLECTIVE SECURITY": NOTES ON THE HISTORY OF AN IDEA

The following monographs are useful as sources of information on certain phases of collective security: Ruhl J. Bartlett, *The League to Enforce Peace* (Chapel Hill, N. C., 1944); Edward H. Buehrig, *Woodrow Wilson and the Balance of Power* (Bloomington, Ind., 1955); Richard N. Current, *Secretary Stimson: A Study in Statecraft* (New Brunswick, N. J., 1954); Robert H. Ferrell, *Peace in Their Time: The Origins of the Kellogg-Briand Pact* (New Haven, 1952); Willard N. Hogan, *International Conflict and Collective Security* (Lexington, Ky., 1955); Harley Notter, *The Origins of the Foreign Policy of Woodrow Wilson* (Baltimore, 1937); and Benjamin M. Ziegler, *The International Law of John Marshall* (Chapel Hill, N. C., 1939).

Among the expounders of the Kellogg Pact are Albert E. Hindmarsh, *Force in Peace* (Cambridge, Mass., 1933); Manley O. Hudson, *By Pacific Means* (New Haven, 1935); James T. Shotwell, *War as an Instrument of National Policy* (New York, 1929) and *On the Rim of the Abyss* (New York, 1936). Expositions of collective security include Maurice Bourquin, ed., *Collective Security: A Record of the Seventh and Eighth International Studies Conferences* (Paris, 1936); C. A. W. Manning, "The Future of the Collective System," in *Anarchy or World Order* (New York, 1936); Quincy Wright, ed., *Neutrality and Collective Security* (Chicago, 1936), which contains the Harris Foundation lectures of Sir Alfred Zimmern and Edwin DeWitt Dickinson; Denna F. Fleming, *The United States and World Organization: 1920-1933* (New York, 1938), which is more a plea for collective security than it is an objective monograph; and Andrew Martin, *Collective Security: A Progress Report* (Paris, 1952), a UNESCO publication. Two recent scholarly works, both of which favor collective security as a means of strengthening the American system of alliances, are Kenneth W. Thompson, "Collective Security Re-examined," in the *American Political Science Review,* XLVII (1953), 753-772, and Henry L. Roberts, *Russia and America: Danger and Prospects* (New York, 1956).

Criticisms of collective security from an isolationist point of view may be found in Edwin M. Borchard and William P. Lage, *Neutrality for the United States* (New Haven, 1937; new ed., 1940), and in Charles A. Beard, *American Foreign Policy in the Making: 1932-1940* (New Haven, 1946). Criticisms from the world federationist point of view are represented by Emery Reves, *The Anatomy of Peace* (New York, 1945; rev. ed., 1946), and by Cord Meyer, Jr., *Peace or Anarchy* (Boston, 1948). Criticisms from a "realist" point of view are in Edward H. Carr, *The Twenty Years' Crisis: 1919-1939* (London, 1939); Hans J. Morgenthau, *Peace, Security & the United Nations* (Chicago, 1946), containing Frederick L. Schuman's Harris Foundation lecture; and Walter Schiffer, *The Legal Community of Mankind: A Critical Analysis of the Modern Concept of World Organization* (New York, 1954).

Chapter 3

MILITARY FORCE AND AMERICAN POLICY, 1919-1939

The relation of American foreign policy to military force has not been the subject of many previous studies. An interesting essay on contemporary aspects of the subject is Henry A. Kissinger's "Force and Diplomacy in a Nuclear Age," *Foreign Affairs,* XXXIV (April, 1956), 349-366. As for more general treatments, Louis Smith, *American Democracy and Military Power* (Chicago, 1951) traces the ideal of civilian supremacy over military matters for the entire period of American history. On military policy in the United States there is much useful information in Gordon Turner, ed., *A History of Military Affairs in Western Society since the Eighteenth Century* (New York, 1953). Another important study of military policy is Mark S. Watson, *Chief of Staff: Prewar Plans and Preparations* (Washington, 1950); the second chapter deals with the period 1920-1940. The essay by Colonel George A. Lincoln, "Military and Strategic Aspects of Contemporary American Foreign Policy," in Alfred H. Kelly, ed., *American Foreign Policy and American Democracy* (Detroit, 1954) is also helpful.

The problem of developing a foreign policy in accord with American ideas and ideals of military force is well stated in William Yandell Elliott, ed., *United States Foreign Policy: Its Organization and Its Control* (New York, 1953); Part III, "Power, Principle, and Policy," is especially valuable. Dexter Perkins has given some interesting interpretations in his *American Approach to Foreign Policy* (Cambridge, Mass., 1952), Chapters 5 and 6 on "The American Attitude toward War" and "The American Attitude toward Peace." John B. Whitton, ed., *The Second Chance: America and the Peace* (Princeton, 1944) is also valuable. In this latter volume Chapter 6, "Public Opinion and the Peace," by Jerome S. Bruner, and Chapter 7, "American Ideals and the Peace," by George F. Thomas, are especially useful. Another interesting general study is Thomas I. Cook and Malcolm Moos, *Power through Purpose: The Realism of Idealism as a Basis of Foreign Policy* (Baltimore, 1954).

Gabriel A. Almond, *The American People and Foreign Policy* (New York, 1950) provides an extensive study of popular influence on the use of force as related to foreign policy. A stimulating work on public opinion and foreign policy during the interwar years is Dexter Perkins, "The Department of State and American Public Opinion," in Gordon A. Craig and Felix Gilbert, eds., *The Diplomats: 1919-1939* (Princeton, 1953).

The debate since 1947 on idealism versus realism as the basic approach to foreign policy throws light on the question of military force and foreign policy. A covenient source for the theories of the idealist and realist is Morton Gordon and Kenneth N. Vines, eds., *Theory and Practice of American Foreign Policy* (New York, 1955). In this latter book, sections 12 through 16 of Part II give the arguments by the leading proponents of the two theories.

Chapter 4

THE PEACE MOVEMENT

The organized peace movement in the United States has been the subject of a number of monographs, but there is as yet no general treatment. Merle Curti, *Peace or War: The American Struggle 1636-1936* (New York, 1936) deals chiefly with the nineteenth century. Arthur C. F. Beales, *The History of Peace* (New York, 1931) likewise is inadequate for the period after 1918. Useful information on the peace movement during the 1920's is in Florence B. Boeckel, *Between War and Peace: A Handbook for Peace Workers* (New York, 1928) and Jerome Davis, *Contemporary Social Movements* (New York, 1930), pp. 747-868. For the decade of the 1930's there is Robert E. Bowers, "The American Peace Movement, 1933-1941," an unpublished doctoral thesis at the University of Wisconsin (Madison, 1947). Supplementary to Bowers's work are two articles by John W. Masland dealing with the peace movement at the end of the thirties: "The Peace Groups Join Battle," *Public Opinion Quarterly*, IV (Dec., 1940), 664-673; and "Pressure Groups and American Foreign Policy," *Public Opinion Quarterly*, VI (Spring 1942), 115-122.

A number of books and pamphlets have been written on special aspects of the peace movement. Notable is the Harvard doctoral thesis (Cambridge, Mass., 1950) by Allen A. Kuusisto on the National Council for Prevention of War—"The Influence of the N.C.P.W. on U.S. Foreign Policy, 1935-39." There are also Lilian Stevenson, *Towards a Christian International: The Story of the International Fellowship of Reconciliation* (3rd ed., London, 1941); Charles S. Macfarland, *Pioneers for Peace through Religion: Based on the Records of the Church Peace Union (Founded by Andrew Carnegie) 1914-1945* (New York, 1946); *Twenty Years of the Foreign Policy Association* (n.p., 1939); "A Brief Review of Thirty-Five Years of Service toward Developing International Understanding," *International Conciliation*, No. 417 (Jan., 1946), 17-39, dealing with the Carnegie Endowment for International Peace. Dorothy Detzer's delightful *Appointment on the Hill* (New York, 1948) records the trials of the Washington lobbyist of the Women's International League for Peace and Freedom. John E. Stoner, *S. O. Levinson and the Pact of Paris* (Chicago, 1942) relates the activity of the American Committee for the Outlawry of War, and will soon be supplemented by a work by J. Chalmers Vinson dealing with the joint activity for peace of Salmon O. Levinson and Senator William E. Borah. Professor Vinson's *The Parchment Peace: The United States Senate and the Washington Conference, 1921-1922* (Athens, Ga., 1955) has chapters concerning the American peace movement and disarmament. The best general volumes on disarmament are by Merze Tate, *The Disarmament Illusion* (New York,

1942) and *The United States and Armaments* (Cambridge, Mass., 1948).

Files of many peace organizations, together with pertinent manuscript collections of personal papers of peace leaders, have been deposited in the Swarthmore College Peace Collection. In the Salmon O. Levinson MSS, desposited in the William Rainey Harper Library of the University of Chicago, there is material of great interest on the peace movement.

Chapter 5

CORDELL HULL AND THE DEFENSE OF THE TRADE AGREEMENTS PROGRAM, 1934-1940

The American Economic Association has sponsored the preparation of two volumes of original essays which review modern developments in various areas of economic theory; each volume is entitled *A Survey of Contemporary Economics.* Volume I (Philadelphia, 1948), edited by Howard S. Ellis, contains "The Theory of International Trade," by Lloyd A. Metzler; and Volume II (Homewood, 1952), edited by Bernard F. Haley, includes "International Investment," by Norman S. Buchanan; both articles review a large mass of literature. For a sympathetic evaluation of international trade theory, see Gottfried Haberler, "The Relevance of the Classical Theory under Modern Conditions," *American Economic Review,* XLIV (May, 1954), 543-561.

Two examinations of the economic causation of war are given by Lionel Robbins, *The Economic Causes of War* (London, 1939) and Jacob Viner, "Peace as an Economic Problem," in his collection of essays on foreign economic policy, *International Economics* (Glencoe, Ill., 1951). One of the few detailed studies of how foreign trade policy has been, and may be, used for purposes of national power is Albert O. Hirschman, *National Power and the Structure of Foreign Trade* (Berkeley, Calif., 1945).

There is a large literature on foreign economic policy in general. An excellent broad survey of problems and policy possibilities is provided by a study group chaired by William Y. Elliott, *The Political Economy of American Foreign Policy: Its Concepts, Strategy, and*

Limits (New York, 1955). Jacob Viner, *International Trade and Economic Development* (Glencoe, Ill., 1952), is a set of lectures on both trade theory and trade policy.

With respect to American tariff history, the outstanding work is Frank W. Taussig, *Tariff History of the United States* (New York, 1931). Asher Isaacs, *International Trade: Tariff and Commercial Policies* (Chicago, 1948) reviews the history of commercial policies of the major trading nations. On the early years of the trade agreements program, the best work is Henry J. Tasca, *The Reciprocal Trade Policy of the United States* (Philadelphia, 1938). A useful source is the United States Tariff Commission, *Operation of the Trade Agreements Program, June 1934 to April 1948* (Washington, 1949), with annual supplements.

While much work has been done on United States tariff history, a relatively neglected aspect is public tariff debates. However, the debates of 1929-1930 are reviewed by Frank W. Fetter, "Congressional Trade Theory," *American Economic Review*, XXIII (Sept., 1933), 413-427. Covering a greater span of time are two articles by William R. Allen, "The International Trade Philosophy of Cordell Hull, 1907-1933," *American Economic Review*, XLIII (March, 1953), 101-116, and "Issues in Congressional Tariff Debates, 1890-1930," *Southern Economic Journal*, XX (April, 1954), 340-355. For further material on Hull, one may consult *The Memoirs of Cordell Hull* (2 vols., New York, 1948).

Chapter 6

AMBIGUITY AND AMBIVALENCE IN IDEAS OF NATIONAL INTEREST IN ASIA

Scholarly studies of the relations of the United States and Asia have for the recent period concentrated primarily on the diplomatic exchanges and given only passing consideration to the ideas and interests which have shaped American policy. Of these, the best is still A. Whitney Griswold's *The Far Eastern Policy of the United States* (New York, 1938), although now in many sections outdated by events and later scholarship. The best general sources for the more recent materials are the last editions of textbooks on Far Eastern relations.

notably those of Donald Lach and the late Harley F. MacNair, and of Paul H. Clyde. At least one specialized diplomatic study deserves mention for its attention to the underlying ideas, that of Dorothy Borg, *American Policy and the Chinese Revolution: 1925-1928* (New York, 1947).

The annual volumes of *Foreign Relations* reveal some of the thinking of policy makers and diplomats, and the State Department archives contain some additional unpublished materials of value, notably John V. A. MacMurray's memorandum of 1935, "Developments Affecting American Foreign Policy in the Far East." The Roosevelt Library at Hyde Park is another essential source for official thought. The published diaries of Harold Ickes, Pierrepont Moffat, and Joseph C. Grew offer valuable glimpses of official thought, and additional important materials can be expected in the unopened papers of Henry Morgenthau, at Hyde Park, and Cordell Hull, in the Library of Congress.

Two official Army histories provide some knowledge of military planning in the late 1930's, Mark S. Watson's *Chief of Staff: Prewar Plans and Preparations* (Washington, 1950) and Maurice Matloff and Edwin Snell, *Strategic Planning for Coalition Warfare, 1941-1942* (Washington, 1953). As well done as are these volumes, naval planning is not their chief concern and is treated only in brief. Naval thought about the Far East in the 1920's has been well covered by Gerald Wheeler's unpublished doctoral dissertation at the University of California, but the next decade awaits study.

Chapter 7

ISOLATIONISM AND COLLECTIVE SECURITY: THE
USES AND LIMITS OF TWO THEORIES OF
INTERNATIONAL RELATIONS

The writings on isolation leave something to be desired. In addition to the titles listed under Chapter I, one can mention William L. Langer and S. Everett Gleason, *The Challenge to Isolation: 1937-40* (New York, 1952); Charles A. Beard and G. H. E. Smith, *The Idea of National Interest* (New York, 1934) and *The Open Door at Home* (New York, 1934); Walter Millis, *The Road to War*

(Boston, 1935); "The Political Philosophy of Young Charles A. Beard," *American Political Science Review*, XLIII (December, 1949), 1175 ff.; Jerome Frank, *Save America First* (New York, 1938); Edwin M. Borchard and William P. Lage, *Neutrality for the United States* (New Haven, 1937; rev. ed., 1940); Oswald G. Villard, *Fighting Years* (New York, 1939); Robert E. Osgood, *Ideals and Self-Interest in America's Foreign Relations* (Chicago, 1953); Richard Olney, "International Isolation of the United States," *Atlantic Monthly*, LXXXI (May, 1898), 577-588.

On collective security, in addition to the titles listed in Chapter II, some of the writings above are useful as well as Hans J. Morgenthau, *Politics among Nations* (New York, 1948); Winston S. Churchill, *The Second World War: The Gathering Storm* (Boston, 1948); Harrop Freeman and Theodore Paullin, *Coercion of States in Federal Unions* (Philadelphia, 1943); Edwin M. Borchard, "The Impracticability of Enforcing Peace," *Yale Law Journal*, LV (Aug., 1946), 968 ff.; Roland N. Stromberg, "The Idea of Collective Security," *Journal of the History of Ideas*, XVII (April, 1956), 250-263; F. Wilson, *The Origins of the League Covenant* (London, 1928); David Hunter Miller, *The Drafting of the Covenant* (2 vols., New York, 1928); Herbert Butterfield, *Christianity, War, and Diplomacy*; Hans J. Morgenthau, *In Defense of the National Interest* (New York, 1952); Raymond Aron, *The Century of Total War* (New York, 1954); Reinhold Niebuhr, *Christian Realism and the Political Problem* (New York, 1955); Francis P. Walters, *A History of the League of Nations* (2 vols., London, 1952); Leland M. Goodrich and Anne Simon, *The United Nations and the Maintenance of International Security* (New York, 1955); and Francis O. Wilcox and Carl M. Marcy, *Proposals for Changes in the United Nations* (New York, 1956). One should also mention occasional writings by Ernest Haas, Howard Johnson, Gerhard Niemeyer, and William W. Kaufmann, including the latter's "The Organization of Responsibility," *World Politics*, I (July, 1949), 511-532. Arnold Wolfer's *Britain and France between Two Wars* (New York, 1940) and William T. R. Fox's *The Super-Powers* (New York, 1944) deal with an earlier period.

Index

Acheson, Dean, U. S. Secretary of State: on collective security, 53-54; mentioned, 133, 136

Adams, George B., historian: quoted, 15

Adams, President John: on libertarian tradition, 161; on treaty with France, 161-162, 163

Adams, John T.: opposes World Court, 72

Addams, Jane, 101

Air Force, Army, 58

America First Committee: backbone of, 20; principles of, 24; mentioned, 105

"America Firsters": and isolationism, 164

American Committee for the Cause and Cure of War, 83, 100, 102, 104

American Committee for the Outlawry of War, 83, 87, 89, 100, 101

American Peace Society: and use of force, 34, 36; mentioned, 82

American Union for Concerted Peace Efforts, 50

Andorra, 94

Anglophiles, 13

Anglophobia: distinctive in isolationism, 31; element of isolationism, 11, 30

Anti-expansionism: in U. S., 164

Antiforeignism: element of isolationism, 11; mentioned, 24

Antimilitarism: basic in isolationism, 31; element of isolationism, 11; of Bryan, 23

Appeal of the Thirty-one, 66-67

Arbitration, 85, 96-97, 102, 105, 106

Argentina, 94

Arms embargo: Kellogg Pact and, 41, 43; see also Neutrality laws

Armstrong, John P.: on Senator Robert A. Taft, 169

Army: U. S., 59-60

Article 10 of League of Nations Covenant: compared to Article 2 of the Four-Power Treaty, 69; rejected by the American people and Senate, 65-

66; Wilson defends, 64-65; mentioned, 10, 68; see also League of Nations

Asia-first vs. Europe-first, 152-157

Association of Nations, 66, 68, 71

Atomic weapons: collective security and, 53; isolationism and, 28

Austria-Hungary: in First World War, 35, 37; mentioned, 91

Axson, Stockton: quotes Wilson, 36

Balance of Power: and Britain, 14, 25; and collective security, 33, 35, 37, 45-46, 52, 55; destroyed by Germany, 8; evils of, 7; and isolationism, 27; and League of Nations, 9; after Second World War, 10

Barnes, Harry Elmer: intellectual isolationist, 21

Bartholdt, Richard: favors compulsory arbitration, 63

Beard, Charles, A.: on collective security, 139; defines isolationism 21; liberal isolationist, 18-19; mentioned, 22; quoted, 11, 23

Belmont, August, New York banker, 139

Bemis, Samuel F., historian, 148

Berger, Victor L., 83

Bliss, Tasker H., 75

Boer War, 12

Bolivia, 94

Borah, William E., U. S. senator: and Arms embargo, 43; begins campaign against World Court, 73; champions Kellogg-Briand Pact in the Senate, 77; and the enforcement of outlawry of war, 74-75; keeps definition of aggressor out of Kellogg-Briand Pact, 76-77; on League, 39; rejects Harmony Plan, 76; rejects military force as a method for preserving peace, 68; and Senate resolution to outlaw war, 75; and World Court, 71-72

Borah Resolution, 1920, 63-64

ATED